HOW TO MAKE

MONEY

FROM PROPERTY

GARY McCAUSLAND

COLLINS & BROWN

To my beautiful daughter, Eva

This edition first published in 2009 by
Collins & Brown
10 Southcombe Street
London
W14 0RA

An imprint of Anova Books Company Ltd

9781843405177

A CIP catalogue for this book is available from the British Library.

10 9 8 7 6 5 4 3 2 1

This book was first published in 2008 as How to Make A Million From
Property.

Typeset by SX Composing DTP, Rayleigh Essex
Printed by Mondadori, Cles, Italy

Keep updated. Email sales@anovabooks.com for FREE email
alerts on forthcoming titles.

This book can be ordered direct from the publisher.
Contact the marketing department, but try your bookshop first.

www.anovabooks.com

Contents

Foreword

If you can keep your head when all about you
Are losing theirs...

If by Rudyard Kipling

As you open this book, you will be asking yourself: 'Can I still become a property entrepreneur when markets seem to be falling all over the world?'. In the earlier edition of this book, I made it clear that the advice I was giving was good for a falling market as well as a rising one. I told you that my twelve-week property plan would enable you to give up the day job, if that was your goal. Since the book came out the world has changed beyond all recognition; in fact, as I write the updates in late 2008, the situation continues to change on a daily basis. But my rules are still just as important for you to follow, if not more so than ever.

I know this because I bought two large sites for property development just before the credit crunch. It should have been a recipe for disaster, because I bought when the market was high, but even on these developments my head is above water and I still expect to make profits. That is because I kept to all of my rules – buying at the right price, buying in a good location where I fully understood the market, and adding value through planning permission.

However, the parameters of the property world have changed – credit is very hard to come by, for example, you can no longer get a 100 per cent mortgage, and there has been a major shift in our financial systems. They have changed forever. Property prices have also changed. Six months ago I was offered a property for £5 million and now it is half the price. You will see similar opportunities and maybe this is the time to act, if you can. However, remember that property, like any other business, has its risks. But as long as you follow the principles in this book, you should still be able to make money. And, because I can't say it too often, those principles are: buy at the right price; make sure you know your location and market; be able to add value; and get the timing right.

The truth is, this has not been a good time for property developers and investors – including myself. It's been a very challenging and difficult time with prices falling, finance freezing up and huge uncertainty at every turn. The government is working hard to bring some stability to the marketplace, but we've got the debt hangover to deal with. All around, developers and small builders are going bankrupt. People have stopped buying land to develop. People have stopped buying houses.

But, remember, property is the backbone of the British economy. All roads lead to property whether it's buying white goods, beds, TVs, DVDs, sofas or even computers. The property industry employs a huge percentage of the workforce directly or indirectly: plumbers, electricians, builders, financiers, mortgage companies, brokers. Now the industry appears to have fallen off a cliff and you might be thinking 'how are we going to get through this?', but there's an old saying in Ireland: 'we haven't died of winter yet', and we won't this time either. We will get through this somehow. In fact, maybe this is one of the best times to start a property business, assuming that you're lucky enough to have the cash! If you haven't got it, don't worry, where there's a will there's a way.

In the long term property is an irresistible investment, and ultimately because of limited supply and increasing demand, it will inevitably go up in value.

In the future we will all have to decide more carefully how to invest our hard-earned cash – whether it is pensions or savings. We could leave it in the bank, which we now know isn't necessarily secure or inflation-proof anymore. We can put it in the stock markets or fancy funds – and we know the risks involved in that, with irresponsible mavericks gambling with our money across the globe. Or we could take our investments into our own hands and look for stability and profit. Bricks and mortar are tangible. It's not going to go anywhere. You can insure it. It's solid, and over the long term a tangible asset remains of value. Property has performed better than stocks and shares in the long term, and what's more you can live in it or collect a rent from it. Demand and supply keep the property market moving

– and demand for housing in parts of the UK is not being satisfied. I believe property is still one of the safest long-term investments you can make. But you have to be careful, keep your eyes wide open – and read on.

This book is for people who need guidance in the property market – whether you are dabbling in it or want to build up a large portfolio. After reading it you might decide not to go into property because it's too risky, or too difficult – make one wrong decision and it can cost you tens of thousands of pounds. If you want to make money at property, you've got to be extremely well informed. This book has all you need.

The property world has changed in just a few months. Developers who I admire and who've been in the business for 50 years are going under right now. No one expected this financial calamity to develop like it has. I admit that it didn't register with me how scary and difficult things would become in the world of property, which is why I've added two new chapters to this book – 'The credit crunch explained' and 'Ten ways to beat the credit crunch'.

I am not going to pretend that becoming a property entrepreneur will be easy, but there is no doubt in my mind that, if you follow the rules in this book, it is possibly one of the best times to get involved in property for many years. So in one way making money from property has never been so difficult, but in another way it's never been so easy, as there are unprecedented opportunities out there if you can raise the finance. I suppose it depends on which view of the world you decide to take. People will look back and say, 'if only I'd bought when prices crashed at the end of the Noughties'. You'll see!

The credit crunch explained

This chapter will explain:

- What happened to the property market

- Why we're in a huge economic mess

- Why it is now hard to find finance & mortgages

- And how you can still make money from property.

Do you remember the last property crash in the 1980s? Well I do! I had left university and, although I wanted to work in property, I couldn't get a job. I ended up doing post-graduate studies and eventually took a job counting sausages in a factory as a trainee accountant – it wasn't my idea of fun, believe me! It was a tough time, and to be frank it is even tougher now. But despite this downturn in the market there is no doubt in my mind that property is still a great long term investment – property markets may go down but they will eventually go back up. It's the basic economics of supply and demand.

What happened to the property market?

Remember this important statistic. Over the last hundred years property, on average, has risen by about 10 per cent per annum. People may be panicking now because prices have dropped 20 per cent in the last few months, and will probably fall some more, but we should remind ourselves that prices had risen 187 per cent in the previous 10 years, before the current downturn. So when we put it into perspective, things actually aren't as bad as people make out. We are due a correction and that's what's happening now; the problem is that the credit crunch has compounded the problems.

Why are we in this huge economic mess?

First, here's the science bit.

In the UK we have had a mixture of events creating what I call the 'perfect storm' in the market place. Property prices reached a peak when at the same time interest rates, costs and inflation were also increasing, and to add insult to injury we were hit with the credit crunch, something most of us had never heard of until recently.

Now we've all read, seen and heard the term in the media so what is the credit crunch? Well, in a nutshell, the 'credit crunch' is a sudden reduction in the general availability of loans (or credit), or the sudden increase in the cost of obtaining loans from banks.

The result was that even banks stopped lending to each other, never mind to us, because they were afraid that they would not get their money back. This resulted in the loss of credit, and to you and me that means more expensive loans and mortgages and the withdrawal of many financial products.

The credit crunch can be traced back to the sub-prime mortgage business in the USA. Sub-prime mortgages are mortgages that carry a higher risk to the lender (and therefore tend to be at higher interest rates) because they are offered to people with poor credit histories or who have low or unpredictable incomes. After September 11th 2001, the US government lowered interest rates to 0.5 per cent to stabilise the economy, and in order to create fees the banks started lending aggressively to virtually anybody so that they could hit their targets and make bonuses. Interest rates were kept too low for too long and the whole system spiralled out of control; money was being lent in its billions to people who would never be able to pay it back.

So when interest rates started to rise again it was a disaster waiting to happen. In many cases people who had borrowed to buy a house had also borrowed money to buy other things – holidays, cars, the latest fashionable accessories. They didn't care how much they had borrowed because they believed that the value of their property was increasing year on year. (Sounds familiar? This has happened in the UK as well.) Ultimately these people did not have the means to repay these loans over the long term.

The banks then took this mortgage debt and bundled it together with other loans to make a financial product known as Asset Backed Securities (or ABSs for short), a portfolio which could then be traded to other banks. Selling these portfolios freed up funds to lend to even more homeowners. The banks who bought these securities received income when the original home-buyers made their mortgage payments.

With credit card debt included in these portfolios the whole thing was becoming a mess – how much was good debt, how much was bad? Control in the lending system had collapsed – the wheels were falling off rapidly but the people in the know were ignoring the warning signs. When house prices then started to fall and interest rates started going up homeowners who couldn't afford to pay back their debt started missing their repayments, leading to a huge increase in repossession levels.

It is important to point out here that the US property market is very different from the market in the UK. There are less strict planning laws. There is so much land they virtually give it away. Apart from prime real estate like Manhattan and Beverly Hills, most of this land is very cheap. The minute homeowners stopped paying the mortgage on their properties, the asset was then almost worthless.

There was no one out there who wanted to buy houses that were worth nothing in a market that had lost the plot; the banks were left with worthless properties. And some of these were UK banks that had bought these Asset Backed Securities from the USA. They were now sitting with billions of pounds of what we now call toxic debt.

As the sub-prime mortgages had been sold and re-sold many times over, the banks simply did not know how much bad mortgage business and toxic debt they had bought. As a result, banks now don't want to lend money to each other and the continuous movement of money, what bankers call liquidity, has dried up. Think of it like playing cards, where you ask the banker to back you because you tell them you have a really good hand. But the banker is afraid that your hand is not as good as you say it is, and thus decides not to lend you any money. You could be bluffing. Banks are looking at each other thinking 'Are you the next Lehman Brothers? Are you the next Northern Rock? Can we trust you with our money?' And time and time again, the answer is 'No'. So they refuse to lend to each other and credit markets freeze. It's a worse case scenario!

Because the banks won't lend to each other anymore, the global economy is effectively starting to seize up. Banks and building societies have been starting to scream out for funds. This hurts our mortgages, credit cards and loans because the banks don't want to lend, but instead want to conserve cash. If that wasn't bad enough, oil and commodity prices have gone up and down and continue to be volatile, creating what the markets hate: uncertainty. There is a huge amount of pain that we all have to deal with because of this, and what's more, it may get worse.

When the world's financial system is short of money it reacts a bit like a human body starved of oxygen. The oxygen keeps the whole system alive. That's why the UK government has pumped £400bn extra capital into several of the UK's largest banks and building societies to keep them going. This is the oxygen they need to survive. Hopefully things will start to recover and stabilise sooner rather than later because every business needs credit and property.

Why is it hard to get credit or find a mortgage product?

It is against this background that the banks and mortgage companies have been struggling. They couldn't keep up with all of their running costs, they couldn't raise money on the market because of all the toxic assets, and the result is that they have become desperate for cash and are hoarding whatever they get their hands on. So now they are refusing loans to people who would previously have got them and the parameters on how they lend have changed dramatically almost overnight.

Today, if you want to secure a mortgage on a property, instead of putting down a typical 5 per cent of the price as a deposit, you have to come up with a minimum of 10 per cent, but more likely 15 per cent, 20 per cent, or 25 per cent. More than that, the bank will expect you to have excellent credit ratings. They will rarely accept anyone on a self-certificated mortgage; they will not take risks. They need cash so they have increased their mortgage rates, and saving rates. They have cut a staggering 70 per cent of available mortgage products. It was these mortgage products that were the lifeblood of the property industry and they were removed in just a few short months. The oxygen has been taken out of the system. The life support machine of the property market has virtually been turned off.

The result is that the government has stepped in, propping up struggling banks, but the banks are still reluctant to pass the deals on to the customers; they want to keep the money in their own accounts. They don't want new business; they just want to get themselves as cash rich as possible and survive this financial tsunami.

Can you still make money from property?

The simple answer is yes, but the biggest challenge right now is getting your hands on the finance.

The property market is taking a hammering. But watch this space. The government is putting pressure on the banks and interest rates will drop further. As I write this chapter they have just dropped to 3 per cent. I expect them to drop as low as 2 per cent in 2009. This should kick-start the market and hopefully free up that all important finance. Prices will drop further and we may see government incentives like relaxing the rules on stamp duty or possible mortgage interest relief. No one knows precisely when the market will turn. If you're lucky and you guess right, you could do very well. If you guess wrong, you could lose even more money. But turn around it will, and it could happen more quickly than anyone thinks.

Warren Buffett, one of the world's richest men and most successful investors, has pointed out recently that there might not be an opportunity like this for another 25 years. He sees lots of scope for investment in the markets and property, but the key is you've got to have the funds available.

The credit crunch is here to stay for some time. Trillions of dollars have evaporated from the market. It's going to take a long time to recover. It is still risky to get involved in property, but if you can find the cash and follow the rules in this book you still should be able to do very well.

I've had a really tough year, but I'm still here. I've survived so far and as this could be one of the best times to buy for the next quarter of a century I'm putting my money where my mouth is – I've just purchased a new development site for 50 per cent of what it was offered to me for 6 months ago. But it's still tough, finance is hard to come by and there's an over-supply of apartments in many cities so property development in many parts of the UK will be patchy for the foreseeable future.

The financial model of how the world works has changed and in a way it is a good thing because it had to change. There was too much greed, too much waste and too much irresponsibility. We are also in the internet age – information travels fast, almost too fast, which has made markets extremely volatile. So governments are re-looking at the financial models to create stability for business in this new era. It's incredibly painful now, but there some positive results to look out for:

1 There are a plenty of motivated sellers in the property market place; in other words there are major opportunities out there.

2 You can find properties that are 25 per cent+ below their earlier value. Many deals are half the price of what they were a year ago.

3 It is getting easier to obtain planning permission as planners are under a mandate to create opportunities for more housing in this time of limited activity.

4 If you can carry on and manage to stay in business (survival rather than profit-making) you will be in a good position when the market recovers.

5 There are signs that finance markets are becoming more liquid, interest rates are dropping and, importantly, LIBOR (the rate at which banks lend to each other) is also dropping. This signals easier borrowing in the future.

6 Property prices will probably continue downwards but we will start seeing green shoots and, from 2010/2011, I suspect we should see healthy property growth again.

To be perfectly frank even with all the doom and gloom, lack of finance and limited activity, I am very hopeful for the future because, as far as I am concerned, property is still the best investment out there .

Ten ways to beat the credit crunch

2009/2010 – The year of the buyer?

There is no doubt about it; things are unbelievably difficult out there right now. People are getting hurt, businesses are going bust – it's a war. This is no time for platitudinous sound bites about the way things are, this is a time for straight talking and practical tips. If you are smart, you will know that this is also a time to retrench, get some serious advice (preferably from me) and mount a new campaign. And if you follow my advice carefully, you will get through this crisis and come out of it stronger, smarter and hopefully still smiling. This is a horrendous time, make no mistake about it, but it is slowly but surely becoming a buyer's market and that gives you a massive advantage because when people are running scared, that is when the opportunities are rife.

Before you get into my top ten tips, it is really important that you read this book thoroughly. Don't flick through it! I sound like an old school headmaster but you need to read it from start to finish. The reason I want to stress this is because, as I've said all along, this book is more about how not to lose money from property than it is about how to make money. All the tips and all the advice that I've laid down have been learnt the hard way. It's only then that I had to become the most resourceful person that I've ever been. It's the hard times that shape us, not the good and I've carried these basic principles throughout my life, continually fine tuning them and as far as I am concerned, they still stand. Always learn from someone who has been there, done it and got the t-shirt – believe me, it's easier than doing it yourself!

So, I just want to start by telling you about the five major principles that are most important if you're thinking about getting into the property market. I'll talk more about these in chapter 5, but they are:

- Price

- Location

- The market

- Timing

- Adding value

1 Price

It may sound obvious, but never rely on what an estate agent tells you. They will always inflate a property's value. So this is what you do – research, research, research. It's easier now because of the internet, but take several hours to have a really good trawl of all the properties for sale around the one you want. Also, go there, walk the streets, take notes of what other properties are on the market and look them up. Comparisons are easier in cities than the country because the streets are pretty uniform, but if you research well, you will quickly see what like can match with like and get a general impression of the true market value. Know your market. It will help you become a tough negotiator. And remember, if you are buying, the ball is very much in your court right now.

This is no time to be sentimental or to pussyfoot around. In this market, you should be paying substantially less than the real market value. How much is substantially? At least 25 per cent (this has increased from 20 per cent). A bargain is essential if you want to get through the next few years.

One thing to look for is a motivated seller; perhaps somebody who's lost a job and may be keen to sell up before repossession hits. The more motivated they are, the better it is for you. Their motivation becomes your discount.

Make sure, then, that you find out why sellers are selling. It's a tough line of questioning, particularly if they are in a tight spot, but don't forget, you may be doing them a favour and relieving them of a burden.

2 Location

The most fashionable areas, as you know, are the ones where everyone else wants to live and the least likely to offer up bargains. You will always be paying a premium at the outset, with very little room for profit. So the best places to look are the areas that are up and coming, on the borders of posher areas. They will always be cheaper and have the potential to go up when better times arrive.

I really like to get inside the minds of potential buyers. Will they care about amenities, like decent public transport and public facilities like parks? Think about schooling prospects. Again, research is the key here.

And keep abreast of demographics. We're an ageing population, so what does that mean? Ease of access, fewer stairs, close proximity to good shopping and no hills – all the things that people want when they get older. Ground floor flats are a premium in some cities now, as are bungalows in the suburbs and the country. But other areas have larger demographics of

families with children. So check it out: don't go in without the
relevant information at your fingertips.

3 The market

When the deal has been struck, the price agreed and the
champagne drunk, can you sell your property as and when you
want to, and for a healthy profit? There is no happy or sure-fire
bet right now. If you go in at the bottom, your assets should rise
that much further when the market recovers. Yet, that doesn't
mean you should wait for what you think may be a trough. An
apparently depressed market may fall yet further. Or, while you're
waiting for it to fall, it may go back up again. Neither you nor I
can control the runaway horse every time.

But if you can get the fundamentals right in the first place, that
should see you through. If you do that, and the market drops by
20 per cent, you ought to be able to handle the situation. And the
UK has the added bonus of there always being an acute shortage
of land (we are an island after all) with a growing population that is
more likely to be single with fewer family groups. You do the maths.

It all goes back to research, research, research (have I emphasised
this enough?) and the best thing to do is to know the market
where you are buying. Look at potential purchasers within your
area. What are their priorities? How eager to buy is each different
group? The state of the market that's right under your nose is
what matters when you're assessing that crucial deal.

*exclusive property buyer in menorca
is unlikely to want lots of land?
...or does this guarantee peace/privacy?*

4 Timing

Timing is everything and nothing in purchasing a property. You
may know the current market very well, but no one, not even
Warren Buffett, can buck all of its trends. Look what happened
during the recent banking crisis. Not many claim to have predicted
such a spectacular crash and quite so suddenly.

But it is a truism that time is money in property, especially if
you're borrowing large sums. Don't forget that interest rates, just
like shares, can go up as well as down and so can building costs. *understand*

So these are the questions that you should be asking at the outset specifically about timing:

Can I/we get our own funding together quickly enough?

You may find you won't be able to raise the money in time for an auction or to fit in with the schedule of the seller. Always check with your lender (preferably beforehand) how long it takes to secure a loan. And get bank/building society approval in advance, if you're intending to buy something at auction.

How long is it going to take to do all the repairs/improvements that we want to do?

Refurbishment may add value to a property and give you an edge in a tough market, but it takes time. Many's a time that investors' precious profits have been whittled away by time spent on making those costly improvements and, at the moment, the time spent selling the property. Try to work it all out before you make the big leap.

Do I/we need to find out the likely length of a wait for planning permission?

Every planning authority is different. So find out how long they might take to approve or reject your plans. You'll have to schedule all of the building works you intend to undertake and calculate whether you can cover all your costs during that period. Don't wear blinkers here. Be realistic. In fact, be ultra conservative. Blind optimism is the downfall of many an investor.

5 Adding value

If your property is getting into negative equity or you're having problems shifting it or if you are sustaining poor valuations on a property, I urge you to add value to that home if you can.

Obviously you need to have some cash, but one of the big ways to add value is to create extra rooms, extend kitchens and realise any kind of potential with your space.

Lofts

The main way to add value is a loft conversion. They can add 15–20 per cent to the value of the house. They cost anywhere between £15,000 and £30,000 and as long as the cost does not exceed the value added, you're in profit. In other words, if you put a loft conversion in at £20,000 and the value it adds to your house is £50,000, well, you're up £30,000 on the value of your property.

Extensions

Whether it's your kitchen, putting in an extra bathroom, or just an extension into your garden, you can add up to 10–15 per cent to the value of your house. Opening up a kitchen and making an extra bedroom is often profitable in flats. A new owner could use the extra bedroom as an office, or rent it out themselves.

Basements

Basements can be expensive. They can cost anything up to £75,000 but they can add between 20–30 per cent value to your home. Again, you've just got to make sure that the cost does not exceed the added value.

Upgrades

If you can't afford to extend, then upgrade. New kitchens can add more than 5 per cent to the value of a home. New bathrooms can add between 4 per cent and 5 per cent. Adding a conservatory is another option and can add up to 10 per cent. And don't underestimate new windows. Any project that the buyer can see they don't have to do when they move in is a plus.

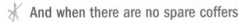

And when there are no spare coffers

Tidying or updating your garden is a clever way to improve the look of your house without spending too much money. As is totally decluttering your home and keeping it very clean and tidy. The last thing you want to do is neglect your asset and let the value start to fall.

Calculating the added value

The best way to work out how much you will be adding is to ask for comparable home prices from your estate agent, or, work out the value by the square footage. For example, if your house is worth £300 per square foot and you put an extra 1,000 sqft extension on, then at £300 per square foot, you've just added £30,000. And also mortgage companies will look at the extra value added and of course a valuer will look at that too.

Planning permission

It is absolutely crucial to know what you can and cannot do to a property BEFORE and not AFTER you close your deal. Let me repeat here, you should make it your business to discover what opportunities will be available from the local authority before signing on the dotted line. Okay, lecture over, but as we've seen, adding value may mean making changes to the property. Use your imagination, but, more importantly, find out if you will get it approved by the local authority. Otherwise, you could be in deep water and out of pocket.

Be bold –  if it doesn't add up, walk away

I know this sounds perverse, but sometimes it's harder to walk away from a deal than stay the course, particularly if you've invested money on surveys, etc. But, believe me; it is essential to walk away from a bad deal in the long run rather than to go ahead. In fact, it is crucial to your survival. So, if you discover that a prospect is not stacking up when you look at some of my bullet points, take courage and call it off. Actually, if it fails on only one of our tests, that should be enough to walk away. Write off the time and money you've spent to experience, or, as I call it, 'school fees'; a credit crunch is not a time to take risks.

Okay, so now you are reacquainted with the basic principles, here are my top tips to beat the credit crunch:

1. Become your own estate agent
2. Sit tight and do nothing
3. Create multiple streams of income
4. Get a partner
5. Find the finance somehow
6. Revise your budget
7. Review your property portfolio
8. Go bankrupt
9. Get advice and find a mentor
10. Stay focused and be strong

1 Become your own estate agent

The great thing about a downturn in the market is that everything is up for grabs. Right now, estate agents are suffering from a lack of stock or inventory while people sit out the crunch. This means that if you are selling, you can barter with them for percentages on their commission. Some have been known to offer their services for as little as 0.5 per cent!

But if you feel let down by estate agents and they aren't getting the results you want, why not do the job yourself? There are lots of benefits of becoming your own estate agent. You get to keep the commission, cut out the middle man and take control of your biggest assets. A lot of research has shown that properties can actually sell faster and for a higher value. The reason is, no one can sell your home like you can!

Now, don't get me wrong, there are lots of good estate agents out there and they are worth their weight in gold, but there are also a fair few bad ones and the property boom over the last ten to fifteen years has created a lot of mavericks who are not to be trusted with your biggest asset. I know, from my own experience in the business, that a lot of people have become disillusioned and want to take matters into their own hands. And I don't blame them. Maybe you are one of them. So here's what to do:

- Keep up appearances. Get your property looking as good as you can. That means making sure the kerb appeal – the outside of the house – is looking as good as possible and that all the junk and clutter is removed, hedges are trimmed, garages are tidied up and all the rooms inside are painted and spotless. You don't have to spend a fortune, but you have to get your property, or product as I call it, looking as good as possible – bright spacious and clean. Research has shown that people decide whether they want to buy a property in the first few minutes of viewing it – first impressions are everything!

- Marketing. You can buy For Sale boards on the internet for about £25 – note that on average 25 per cent of all house sales are instigated entirely through the For Sale sign. This figure rises considerably if you're located on a busy road. So, get your sign up, and then get to work. You can build a website where you can advertise your property with photographs and descriptions – there are also many free property sales sites that you can advertise on. Then there's word of mouth, newspaper ads, local supermarkets, post offices, universities, transport hubs, hospitals, hotels, councils, libraries – the options are pretty limitless. Make a leaflet, spending time on good photographs that display the property in all its glory, then take a weekend to distribute your leaflets and put up posters. You've got to do credible marketing to get your property out there and then you've got to get your viewings. And the key is to remember that people are not just buying a house, they are buying a solution to their problems, a lifestyle, a convenience, proximity to good schools – whatever their motivation, you've got to make sure that your home fits with what they want and that means, when you get people to come to your house and view it, you need to make sure that you know as much about your potential purchaser as possible. So get as much information as you can on the phone without scaring them away. And remember don't oversell. A lot of people in the UK try to oversell and you've got to be quite relaxed.

- Wording of copy. Be straightforward. Most people don't like florid language and hyperbole. Keep the description of your home factual but respect what you have. Mention details like fireplaces, paint effects, lights and other fixtures that are included in the sale, cornicing, wood floors – all the things that sound attractive and that make a property stand out from the rest. Give measurements and a brief description of each room. If you need more guidance, go to some of the estate agents' web sites and see how they present their properties. Whatever you do don't exaggerate or tell falsehoods, this could land you in hot water.

- Photos and videos. For photographs – a wide-angle lens works best. It makes rooms look bigger. Always stand in the corner of a room through a doorway if possible – that way you give the impression of the room being bigger than it is. It goes without saying that when you take the photograph, make everything as spruce as possible – beds made, throws folded, cushions plumped, towels stacked, candles lit, lights on, fires burning – everything you can do to make the home look cosy and inviting. You might even make a video for a web site. Keep it simple. Never zoom in on things. Keep the camera on legs or rest it on something to keep the shot steady and pan slowly around the room. Don't try to be fancy here. It won't get you any brownie points. Keep the shots short too. No more than 12–15 seconds per room.

- Viewings. Always welcome viewers with a smile, regardless of what meets you at the door. Take people through at a steady pace, have all the answers, get information from them, ask them questions and make the first and last rooms entered the ones that count. Make sure they're the best two rooms in the house, because first and last impressions are what people will remember. Don't rush a viewing. Give the potential buyers time to inspect if possible and provide them with privacy if they want it, and, I repeat, don't oversell. When people do come around, make sure there are good smells in the house. The old adage of bread in the oven and coffee on the stove does make a subliminal difference, even fresh lemon cleaning fluid (if your current choice doesn't smell pleasant, change the brand) or pot pourri in the bathrooms. Anything you can do to make your home look and feel like it has been loved and well cared for by you and will be again by the purchaser.

So, at the end of all that effort, you just might find that you've sold your property. You've saved thousands of pounds on estate agents' fees, you've sold it faster and you've actually taken control of your destiny by taking control of your biggest asset. There's nothing worse in a market like this than feeling helpless and having no control – so why not join up with thousands of other people who are taking this route and do it yourself!

2 Sit tight and do nothing

I have developer friends who think it's best to do absolutely nothing. They have been known to virtually mothball their portfolios, rent out everything they can for whatever money they can get, take to the country and sit it out. My old friend Donald Trump is someone who believes in the 'do nothing' philosophy. He has often said: when times are tough, the best thing to do – is do nothing. And what he means is, don't try to sell in a falling market. Don't try to force things. If you can just sit tight, pay the bills and let the storm pass, the storm will always pass. Eventually. What goes down will come back. You see a lot of cases and examples of people cutting their losses and panicking and selling only to find out that a year or two down the line, the market has recovered and if they'd just kept a cooler head, they would be sitting on a lot more money. For instance, I know a guy who decided to sell a huge portfolio, as it turned out, at the very bottom of the market. Three weeks later, the market had improved slightly and he'd just cost himself over a million pounds! So I say, don't follow the sheep mentality. It's so easy to listen to the doom and gloom merchants. I promise you this too will pass, especially in property. Property is incredibly resilient and it will bounce back over the long term. Where would you rather have your market, in stocks and shares and funds? Or in a solid, tangible asset like property?

I know that it's very, very hard to sit and let your legs swing when everything seems to be crashing down around your ears, but if you can make sure you pay your mortgage and keep on top of things, it may be the best choice for you right now. There is a famous quote:
 'Patience is a bitter vine which bears sweet fruit' and it does!

3 Create multiple streams of income

If you look at any multi-millionaire, they usually have several sources of revenue. They never put all their eggs in one basket and there are many simple things you can do to increase your streams of income. Be flexible. Be brave. Be creative. It could save you thousands of pounds. Not to mention your portfolio, or even your home.

If you're really struggling to pay the bills right now, take a deep breath and rent out your property for what you can get for it and move in to one that's cheaper, one you can afford more easily. It's harsh, but it may be necessary. And remember; right now you are not alone. What I'm trying to say here is rather than sit around and not be able to pay the mortgage and face possible repossession, you may have to make a big decision, but it will mean that you keep your house or investment in the long term. By renting out your home to someone who can pay more, it allows you to make sure that your debt is financed until the crisis has eased. There's lots of ways to rent out. You can use agents who will take a 10–15 per cent fee, or you can just be your own estate agent again. Same rules apply as above.

Another way to find some extra cash is to take a lodger. In the UK, you can get tax relief on lodgers and receive up to £4,250 per annum in rent with no tax to pay whatsoever. So that is pure income and if you've got a house that you're working on and you've had to lay down tools for whatever reason, get one of the rooms sorted and get a lodger in. Sometimes it's not fun sharing your space but, you know, in times like this you have to do what you have to do.

There are other ways to lease out your space. You can rent out your car parking spaces at the front of your house to neighbours or companies, depending on where you live. There may be big events happening near you – see if you can rent your house for a week or two to tourists while you go and stay with a friend. Find out what colleges and universities or training hospitals there are in your area and rent out to students. Or summer students who are here for a short stay. If you live in the country, consider doing a bed and breakfast, if you have lots of rooms. Or in town for that matter. Be imaginative: take advantage of the visitors who come here every year. Or use your property as an unofficial community centre, hold meetings to sell things, become a childminder if you are at home with kids, let out a room to a writer or artist as an office/studio – it is amazing who needs space and will pay for it.

The analogy I like to use is that of a bus on a treacherous mountain road. These are impossible times but you have to keep the bus on the road at all costs; you can't fall off the edge. Even if the wheels are rattling, the brakes don't seem to be working, and everyone on the bus is misbehaving, you've just got to keep it as steady as possible. We can sort out the wheels, mend the brakes and throw the misbehaving passengers off the bus at a later stage, but right now keep the bus between the hedges! Keep your life and business on track, keep them on the road.

4 Get a partner

I don't mean a love match, but that could work too! Seriously, I'll give you an example of what has happened to me. Some of the bigger schemes that I've been working on lately have hit major stumbling blocks in terms of financing. It's a case of how do we build them when the banks have said they're not lending to anyone, especially in property? Impasse. And many people will go under. So what I've had to do is to go around trying to find partners and people who will come in with me, bring their skills and expertise and hopefully put some money into the pot as well, and rather than keeping all the profit, I'm going to have to split it with them. But the way I look at it is that I'd rather have a part of the cake than no cake at all. I am prepared to share right now and keep the wheels on the bus.

The people who survive this current downturn are going to be the winners in the future and my number one objective right now is to survive. I have been doing things that I never thought I'd do. I've been linking up with partners who I never thought I'd join forces with – even old enemies – but they, just like me, need good partners to make sure that they survive the credit crunch and in turn it means that I too will survive. They bring different skills & resources to the party. I bring different skills & resources to the party. It's a win/win. We all know that in the long term it will get better and we know that we've got to keep going, so it's a case of getting in bed with a partner, creating a joint venture with them, starting a new company and riding out the storm. Maybe, for you, it will mean approaching a friend, a family member, a business colleague, a mentor, someone you know, and you say look, I've got this huge profit at the end of the line, but what I am prepared to do now is give you a percentage of the profit, if you invest. Then, the negotiation starts. Don't give away your shirt at this point. In fact, go and look at my section on negotiation which has some great tips. But it's a case of – don't get out, get a partner. So start looking now – your business may depend on it.

5 Find the finance somehow

It's the people who come up with creative ways to finance their businesses and schemes who will do well and survive and prosper in these crazy times. I'll give you six ways to get your hands on money:

- You can be given it or inherit it
- You can win it
- You can marry it
- You can steal it
- You can earn it
- You can borrow it

If you inherit it, you're lucky. If you win it, you're one in fifteen million. If you marry it, you're smart. Let's hope they are also good in bed! If you steal it, good luck. You can probably expect a knock on the door in the middle of the night at some point. If you earn it, congratulations in this climate. So what are we left with? What we've always been left with – borrowing. You have to find someone who will take a chance on you, someone who will lend you the money.

We all know that the mortgage world has utterly changed and the days of 125 per cent mortgages are a thing of the past and we may never see their like again. In fact, you will probably be struggling to get even a 90 per cent mortgage these days, but the people who come up with clever ways to raise money are going to be the people who are the big winners in the future. So somehow you've got to look at ways to find money. I know it sounds impossible right now but believe me, the banks need to lend money in order to make a profit. Mortgage companies need to grant mortgages in order to thrive. These products will come back. Liquidity will return to the marketplace. So my advice is – be ready, because it'll come back faster than anyone thinks. It's the oxygen of our system and within the next couple of years, we will see things get better and better on the whole finance front. Just be prepared to move quickly when it does. And in the meantime, be creative in getting what you can in place to survive or indeed move before anyone else does. There are lots of lucky people out there who still have pots of money squirreled away. Perhaps you can convince them to part with some? Go and look at my chapter on finding the finance, 'Get your hands on the money' – it's more important now than ever!

6 Revise your budget

This is a top tip that all entrepreneurs need to implement in a credit crunch. It does not just apply to property, but to every business. You need to revise your budgets, and not just your business budget but also your personal budget as well. It is only when you have control of all outgoings that you can be completely confident about your business and, to be frank, your life.

The place to begin is with your personal budget. Look at the chart opposite for guidance. Your personal budget will pinpoint exactly how much you have coming in and what is going out every month. Start with your income and make sure you include every available source, for example: wages, child support, rent, alimony, disability allowance, pension etc. Write down all your sources of income on a monthly basis and show as your monthly gross income. Then consider every penny that leaves your account. A good way to work this out is to look at your bank statement. There will be regular income deductions like taxes, life insurance and saving plans; and then there will be the unavoidable expenses of rents and mortgages and utility bills. Take a good hard look at what goes out on credit cards. Work out how much you are spending on bills and what you pay out for entertainment and food and transport. You need to factor everything in and examine every part of it. Write it all down or better still put in a spreadsheet and then at the bottom you will get a balance, which will either be a plus or a minus. In most cases, unfortunately, it's a minus.

The next step is to go back over every single item and review it. Ask yourself some hard questions: do you really need to spend X on eating out, do you need to spend X on the car? Could you sell it or get a cheaper deal? Can you cut back on groceries or online services? Could you take in a lodger? The underlying point of all this is to see what your real income is, and then work out how you can make sure that it covers your outgoings.

This is important because you need to be financially stable in order to grow your business. You've got to make sure that you can weather the storm of a long downturn in our economy. If you can keep your personal outgoings under control, you will be in a better position if you need cash for your business. I always say that it's so vital to make sure your own personal situation comes first, because if its chaos at home and you aren't paying the bills the business will suffer even more so. Your home is your base, your oasis, your platform to create a successful business – make sure it comes first!

Monthly Gross Income (salary, child support, pensions, social security, etc.)	
Income deductions: Taxes (income tax and local rates)	
Savings plan and pension	
Insurance (health, life, dental, opticians)	
Total income deductions	
Monthly net income	

Expenses:

Rent or mortgage	
Other housing costs (property taxes, home insurance, etc.)	
Utilities (water, electricity, phone, broadband)	
Travel (train, bus or taxi)	
Car upkeep (petrol, insurance, parking)	
Food – include your restaurant expenses	
Clothes (add dry cleaning here)	
Entertainment (holidays cable, satellite, DVD and VHS rentals, theatre)	
Debt (credit cards)	
Other monthly expenses (child care, gym, pets etc.)	
Total expenses	
Amount left over to save or invest	

After you've worked out all your personal budgets:

- What's coming in?
- What's going out?
- What's the balance?
- What can you cut back on?
- What's your overall final income (and can you increase it)?

Then look at your businesses. Every project you have underway needs a properly planned budget. Make more lists. This time you may well not have any money coming in and plenty of it going out. So, whatever the property, the project – whether you're refurbishing it, whether it's rental income, a buy-to-let or your own home – ask yourself how much you have left in your budget to spend, and then look at how can you shortcut some of the expenditure. The idea is to cut back, trim, manage and revise your budget as much as possible.

It's time to be lean and mean!

It's extremely important to keep a tight check on every single penny. Ask yourself some key questions. What really needs to be done? What must be spent immediately and what could you hold off spending until times are better? Every penny spent must increase the value of your investment. There are cheaper options to consider:

- Instead of putting in wooden floors you can put in laminate floors.
- Instead of putting in that really expensive Philippe Starck kitchen, can you put in a Homebase kitchen?
- Buy cheap kitchen carcasses and add better quality fronts.
- Opt for ceramic tiles instead of marble tiles.
- Paint the interior all the way through in the same clean, unifying colour to create space and save on paint and wallpaper.
- Choose plain white bathroom furniture. It's cheaper, will look more expensive and it won't date.

There are two key questions to ask:

- What can you do to bring the costs down?
- How can you finish the project and get an income faster?

Perhaps you should consider renting your property cheaper for now, or selling for less, just to get money through the door. Look at all of this critically: what's coming in, what's going out?

To make this effective you've got to do it right across the board if you are going to survive and make money in a credit crunch.

It is not all bad news. The downturn has also brought about some positive changes that you can and should take advantage of.

Labour and raw materials are coming down in price. China is not utilising as much steel or as much concrete as first envisaged; and as we've seen, oil prices have recently dropped. Worldwide demand for building materials, including labour, is falling. The UK construction industry is at one of its all-time lows and it's not going to get better anytime soon. So, you can get cheap labour, cheap plumbers, and cheap electricians to help develop your property. Six months ago, you couldn't get hold of these people for love nor money. Right now they're calling me relentlessly.

A glance at your local high street will reveal opportunities for bargains. I recently noticed a kitchen manufacturer going into receivership: they were selling all their kitchens at cut prices. In the centre of town I saw that a lighting shop had a closing down sale; everything was 30 per cent off, 50 per cent off, or even 70 per cent off. I don't like to see anyone go under, but unfortunately that's life, and it gives you the opportunity to buy things cheaply and make sure that you don't go under yourself.

- Look out for bargains; what we call 'motivated sellers'. People who are prepared to get rid of stock at low, low prices.

- A downturn will also bring out motivated people who want to work; and they're often prepared to work for half of what they were paid last year.

- Read chapter 11 – 'Project manage your site'. If you read it in two minutes, look at the detail again slowly and read it properly!

- Get two or three quotes for everything, especially raw materials. You've got to negotiate hard.

- Use your time and energy to save cash, searching for bargains.

- You are fighting a war here. Don't forget it!

I don't want to sound too mercenary but I want to convince you that you've got to be tough. This is no time for dilly-dallying about.

You've got to get out there. You've got to negotiate hard. Go back and revise your budgets; go back and negotiate with your builders, with your suppliers of materials, with everyone. You've got to look at every single avenue to keep the costs low. Look at the chapter on negotiation and really push the boundaries: get your prices down.

This is what I do in my businesses. I track each and every penny in and out of my accounts – both personal and business. People often have a fear of examining their accounts and working out budgets. Inevitably you always spend more than you think, and these figures can reveal some frightening shortfalls. But in order to stay secure and in order to succeed in business you have to look at every single figure. Follow the advice in this chapter – study your bank statements for the last few months, pull out every direct debit, every standing order, look at an average of how much you spend on entertainment, on holidays. Force yourself to make some tough decisions for the sake of your business. Perhaps even for the sake of your survival.

Working out your budgets will also enable you to approach the bank with a sound projected cash flow for your business. Banks are willing to work with you if they can see a sensible business plan.

After analysing your budgets carefully ask yourself three questions:

1 Does your business need a cash injection? If so, how much?

2 Can your business survive over the long term?

3 Are you going to make a profit or a loss?

Now you are in a position to review your property portfolio and restructure accordingly.

7 Review your property portfolio

Take a long, hard look at what investments have made sense and what investments haven't. I live by the rules I've put in this book – and in the credit crunch I have lost a lot of asset value. But my business remains successful because I've followed the key rules and taken tough decisions.

Make an urgent and immediate review of what you're doing in your portfolio even if its only one property, it's still your portfolio right now! If you can chop out things that are costing money, then get rid of them. Now could be the time to sell things to bring in some much-needed cash. You may have to sacrifice a couple of good investments or developments, to get through this in the long run. There's no point in going under because you didn't want to sell a couple of great properties. Believe me, if you run out of money the bank will happily sell them for you, and they'll accept a lot less than you will.

We're probably in one of the worst economic slumps since 1929. This is going to be deep. Yes, there are opportunities out there, but this isn't going to be over today or tomorrow. So you need to review your portfolio in a critical frame of mind. You have to look at it in the cold light of day. If it comes to it, sell what you've got, or strip out what's necessary in order to get through to the next stage when you can make money again.

You may have to look at properties that aren't creating revenue and cut your losses and sell. Other properties may present opportunities that are just so phenomenal, you will find a way to hold onto them. To increase your portfolio you might have to sell some properties in order to buy others. This portfolio review will enable you to understand your strengths and eliminate your weaknesses. It's 'quid pro quo'. You're giving away some things in order to get benefits from others, which will help you survive in this current downturn.

If, after reviewing your portfolio and budget, you are still struggling to find cash, then it is essential to understand and manage your debt responsibilities.

Some of you reading this book may be seriously in debt. It happens. I've done seminars where people have broken down in tears because they're in so much debt. It's a horrible place to be.

There is one thing you mustn't do, and that is bury your head in the sand. Believe me, there is no hiding from the day of reckoning, because the bailiffs really will come knocking on your door. These guys are ruthless. They'll come and take your car and your house; they'll take anything they can get their hands on. So - you have to take action.

Pick up the phone and speak to your mortgage company to let them know that you are in arrears and struggling. Speak to the Citizens Advice Bureau (CAB) or the National Debt Helpline. You can get immediate advice and it is free and confidential. Find your local CAB in the phone book or on the web. National Debtline has a helpline on 0808 8084000. Remember, these people are on the other end of the phone, and they are there to help you. Don't put it off. Speak to people immediately. Right away. In fact if you are in serious debt put this book down now and call the helpline; the sooner you do this the sooner you are on the road to sorting out your life and business. There are also many different debt agencies. But beware of the loan sharks: these are people who are trying to get you to restructure the debt and who will actually force you into more debt. Take professional advice and be very careful.

The trick is to manage your debts. Go back to credit crunch tip seven and work out your monthly cash flow and your weekly cash flow. Understand what comes in through the door and what goes out of it. Look at the weak links and the shortfalls and see if there is anything that you could change to improve the situation. How can you increase income, how can you reduce debt?

The most important thing is to recognise that you have got into difficulties and to take action. It is when people go into a state of denial that the situation escalates out of hand. It may seem hard but you have to open your post, look at your bills, and study your bank and credit card statements. Then talk to the relevant people: the credit card companies and banks. Renegotiate with your mortgage company; ask for a payment holiday. There are also new schemes now where the mortgage company can buy your property or take some equity in it, and rent it back to you. To your surprise you will discover that the people you owe money to will want to help you. They don't want to increase the debt. They don't want to send you to court because they would rather work with you and help your business find its feet again.

8 Go bankrupt

This is a tough tip to give, and very controversial, but it may be the answer. I have a couple of good friends who purchased properties that were bad investments. I told them so at the time but they wouldn't listen – they were caught up in the property boom frenzy. They broke every rule in the book: they paid too much, chose the wrong location, they didn't know the market, and they didn't add value. The upshot was that they were left with properties that no one else wanted. As the property market dropped there was no way out for them, however hard they worked. These friends recognised that it was time to cut their losses and start again as they could never repay their debts. Going bankrupt gave them that fresh start.

Obviously, it is a worst-case scenario. I would not advise anyone to go bankrupt unless it was absolutely necessary. But if you have to do it, then you will find that it's not as bad as most people think. You don't need to feel shame: a lot of very successful businessmen have gone bankrupt. In fact, an alarmingly high percentage of entrepreneurs and business people have had to go bankrupt at some point.

I've counselled and mentored various friends through the process of bankruptcy, and in each case it was the embarrassment of going bankrupt that caused them the most pain and heartache. But they all agreed that once they had done it, they felt released. They could actually get on with their life again.

What it means in reality is that, for a typical period of one year, you're not allowed any credit facility and you lose control of your assets. If you live with a partner or children, then you will usually be allowed a period of time to make other living arrangements, so you may not have to sell your home immediately. You're allowed to keep your income and your personal possessions. So, it's not as bad as it sounds.

Of course, I'm not condoning people going bankrupt. However these are very difficult times, and this is credit crunch advice – if you're in too deep, if there's absolutely no way out, don't go through all that agony, just go and see a solicitor, declare bankruptcy and start afresh. Give yourself a second chance.

For more details, there's the government web site www.directgov.co.uk. The key point of bankruptcy is that it can be a way of clearing debts you can't pay. When you're bankrupt, your property and possessions are used to pay off people that you owe money to. At the end of the bankruptcy period, which is usually a year, most debts are cancelled. If you owe someone over £750 (unsecured) they can start proceedings against you, and if possible you should try and reach a settlement before their 'petition' is heard in court. It is my view that it is better to file your own bankruptcy petition, using a form downloaded from the Insolvency Service website. Then you take the form to the county court nearest to you that has bankruptcy jurisdiction. You will need to pay a deposit of £345, for the Official Receiver to be appointed to protect your assets. They act as trustee of your bankruptcy affairs if you have no assets. Once a bankruptcy order has been made against you, your creditors can no longer pursue you for payment.

I've included some key points from that web site here:

How bankruptcy affects you

Assets

Once you're bankrupt, the Official Receiver, or appointed trustee, can sell your assets to pay your creditors. However, certain goods aren't treated as assets for this purpose, for example:

- Equipment you need for your work (such as tools or vehicles)
- Household items needed by you and your family (such as clothing, bedding and furniture)
- Earnings

The Official Receiver can look at your income (taking into account expenses such as your mortgage, rent and household bills) and decide if payments should be made to your creditors. You might be asked to sign an 'income payments agreement' to pay fixed monthly instalments from your income for three years. If you don't pay (or if you don't sign the agreement voluntarily), the Official Receiver can apply for an income payments order from the court to order you to pay – running for at least three years from the date of the order.

If your circumstances change, you'll need to tell the Official Receiver, so they can review these arrangements.

Ongoing commitments

You'll still have to meet ongoing commitments such as rent or debts incurred after you become bankrupt.

Your obligations when you're bankrupt

You must:

- Give the Official Receiver details of your finances, assets and creditors
- Look after your assets and hand them over to the Official Receiver with the relevant paperwork, such as bank statements and insurance policies
- Tell your trustee (either the Official Receiver or insolvency practitioner) about any new assets or income during your bankruptcy
- Stop using credit cards and bank or building society accounts
- Not obtain credit over £250 without telling the creditor that you're bankrupt
- Not make payments direct to your creditors (there are exceptions to this, such as mortgage arrears and outstanding child support payments)
- You may also have to go to court and explain why you're in debt.

It's worth remembering that a lot of people have been through similar difficulties before, for example in the crash of the 70s. History has a habit of repeating itself. We're in a downturn now; but there'll be a boom again, just as there'll be a downturn again. That's the way it goes. It goes up. It goes down. And no matter how hopeless things seem there are always various courses of action open to you. Don't become a victim of your own passivity. Take control of the problem and if all else fails, go bankrupt. It might just help you start again.

9 Get advice and find a mentor

Paul Walch?
CNB

I have always advocated the benefits of having a mentor. In times of trouble, if you have a mentor, go straight to him or her to get some immediate and independent ideas & strategies. Advice from someone who has already survived financial difficulties and other slumps is an invaluable asset.

If you don't have a mentor, these are the characteristics you are looking for:

- Proven track record of success

- Experience in business (someone who's been there and done it)

- An inspiring, possibly charismatic personality (someone who encourages you to go to the next level)

- Authority (someone who you naturally look up to)

Many experienced business people enjoy helping new entrepreneurs. Also, you can pay for mentors, who like a consultant or a psychologist, offer their services. You go in and tell them your business problems and they'll give you their advice. Ideally, your mentor will also be someone who has weathered the hard times as well as enjoying the good times will have gathered plenty of wisdom and will be a useful ally and advisor. There are also local government business centres, and some banks can offer small business advice too.

Or, if you wanted to approach someone that you admire for advice, you could try sending an email or a letter explaining that you are an entrepreneur, and that you would value his or her advice. But if you don't know them personally, or they haven't offered their advice for a fee, then you will be lucky to get much more than a polite acknowledgement back. For example, I get lots of similar requests, literally thousands of requests for advice, and I can't deal with them all. I'll always send back an email, but it's usually a very short one. So if you know someone personally, that's obviously the best option, as hopefully, that person will be able to offer you individual advice.

Of course, if you can't find a mentor in person, you can always go onto the internet to look for someone. There are various inspirational gurus out there, for example Tony Robbins, Paul McKenna and Greg Secker. Read their books, go to their courses, learn from them. Take a look at a selection of business moguls on YouTube giving their advice, top tips and inspirational talks. Decide who you find most convincing and most inspiring. You will learn more from the people you respect. There are plenty of advice manuals on the bookshelves and it's always useful to see what they have to say; and you can buy books on inspirational figures like Richard Branson, Donald Trump or Duncan Bannatyne. At some point all of these big success stories have hit hard times and have learnt through experience. As you read, try to home in on any tales of difficulty and hardship and glean as much as you can both from their mistakes and from the tactics that have worked for them.

We all need to keep learning from other people. There is always something new to discover. And that's why I personally love reading autobiographies of all the greats – from Donald Trump and Nelson Mandela to Bill Gates. I'm interested in anyone who has done really well in business or life, because it's quicker and easier to learn from them than learn it yourself the hard way. So take my advice and get a mentor – fast!

10 Stay focused and be strong

There is no doubt that this is a challenging time for every industry. Recession soon becomes a depression. And it can become soul-destroying.

My belief is that as long as you are reasonably fit and healthy, you can manage almost anything. Money is without doubt important for the basics in life but it's not everything. Yes, we all want to succeed and make plenty of cash, but sometimes it is necessary to get things into perspective and make sure your values are in the right order. Your life, and the life of the people you love, is the most important thing. Try and help other people; find a charity that you can give your time to. Acknowledging how lucky you actually are in comparison with many other people will help you to understand that if you go bankrupt or things don't work out, it's not the end of the world. There are worse things that can happen – in fact, all over the world, every day, there are worse things happening.

Whatever happens, there is a means to help you. You'll be able to get a roof over your head somewhere. You'll be able to have nice clothes. You'll still be able to have a decent quality of life. You have your friends, your family and most importantly you will have the chance to bounce back. That's the great thing about this country – there is always a second chance. Remember, most people who have gone bankrupt and faced hardships are the ones who become the massive success stories of the future. The message is: you've got to be strong in these hard times. Stay fit and healthy, get to the gym and work out your frustrations there, eat well and stay mentally strong. Stay focused. And don't put your head in the sand; look at the all facts in the cold light of day and know exactly where you are financially.

You also need to recognise that a credit crunch can stretch relationships to breaking point. There's a saying that when money goes out of the door, love goes out the window. Research on marital problems and relationship problems have revealed that 80 per cent of them are caused by money, finances and discussing finances; all the squabbling over who pays for this and who pays for that. So if your partner's not supporting you, I think you have to sit down and have a real big heart to heart with them on the situation. Talk about where you are and what you're both going to do. I always find that as long as you look at the facts you can make a plan. If you don't know where you are in your finances you can't make a plan. You need to make sure that your partner understands your finances as well as you, and that they feel included in every decision and involved in the business. It is essential to present a united front and to offer support to each other. And if your partner is really unable to do this, then it may be time to face this issue, the people you love have to support you through the bad times as well as the good and that's the bottom line.

In summary, in order to remain focused on your business you need to be as fit as possible, positive and determined. This is not a keep fit book, but you will know how to stay healthy. It also helps if you support other people who are worse off than you are. Looking after other people gives you clear evidence of how good your own life is, even when things are not going well.

So there you have my top ten tips. I hope they help you get through this current downturn – and remember, the darkest hour comes before dawn.

As I write this we are witnessing the property market slowly turning into a buyer's market. In some cases businesses, mortgage companies, individuals are desperate to get rid of property. I've always said that I'm the last person to want to see anyone go under, but it's a sad fact of life. With the best will in the world, there's not a lot that can be done. These people are the reason the market is falling. What this means is that there are more motivated sellers right now than I have ever seen in my career. People have taken on too much debt, they've been caught in the buy-to-let trap, or they've had their property repossessed and taken to auction. Ultimately this unfortunate set of circumstances is now your opportunity – and if you don't take that opportunity, someone else will. It's better to make the best of something going wrong and turn it from a bad situation into a good situation than to do nothing, let it fester and let it become a lose/lose scenario.

At the end of the last property crash in the 1980s, anybody who understood the situation went out and somehow raised the finances and bought property. Everyone marvelled at how clever they were. People will look back ten years from now and really regret that they did not buy properties at the end of the Noughties – and again, they will marvel at the people who did.

The UK population is growing, the UK is incredibly resilient. A lot of foreigners still want to live here and there will be a demand for property again. Make no mistake about it, property will bounce back.

Property will always find its value in the long term. The reason is basic economics: we've only got a finite amount of land to build on. We've got to keep the green areas. The human race and populations continue to grow rapidly and thus with limited supply and rising demand, prices will ultimately increase. It's that simple.

The volatile funds of the stock market are also creating demand for property – investors are taking a view that a tangible asset like property is a better long-term bet than stocks and shares. Where would you rather have your money? In a bank like one of those Icelandic offshore accounts, in stocks and shares or in a property in the UK that you can rent out or sell? I'd rather have my money in a tangible property any day of the week. No one can take that from you (as long as you keep paying the mortgage if you have one). And while you wait for its value to increase it can provide an income through the rental market. In terms of investment, property has a bright future.

To be frank this is the moment to make the most of a buyer's market. The opportunities are starting to appear and will improve in 2009 and possibly 2010. There will be a turning point. There'll be a point where the press will report 'Hold on, last month prices just went up by 3 per cent', and then there'll be a stampede. It's always easier to buy in a falling market than it is in a rising market. You can very rarely predict when the bottom is going to be. Many people will move when the curve is starting to go up, but there will be fewer motivated sellers at that point.

Believe it or not, even as I write this book, I'm seeing shoots of recovery and phenomenal buying opportunities. As more mortgage products come back into the market and finance starts to loosen up and things start to get better people are making moves. Right now, individuals who have got cash are negotiating and starting to buy properties. Its going to be a long road to recovery and maybe only the brave are dipping their toe in the water right now but one thing is for sure they are buying property at a lot cheaper than they were a year ago.

So my advice to you is, whatever your reason for resisting – perhaps you've been burnt now or because things have been tough – don't walk away entirely from property. It is still one of the best investments you can ever make long term and there's still lots of opportunities (if not more than ever) to make your million. But make sure you follow the principles in this book. Buy at the right price, in the right location, from a motivated seller, understand your market and add value, watch your budgets and get the timing right. If you do this, when the market does turn, you could end up very rich indeed.

Now it's time to read the rest of this book very carefully!
Good luck...

Making it happen

...can I really make a money from property?

Most people want to get rich and so they should. Money gives you independence and financial security. It allows you to help people and to fulfil your potential as a human being. In the UK and Ireland one obvious pathway to prosperity is in front of your eyes. Our nation's wealth accumulates in the bricks and mortar within which we live and work. It's all around us, we can reach out and touch it. We all know that some people have made huge fortunes by exploiting the opportunities that property holds out and the reason you are holding this book in your hand is because you have asked yourself, 'Can I do the same, can I turn bricks and mortar into serious cash?' The answer is YES. You want to make money and this book will show you how.

Of course, if you become a homeowner, your real worth may well rise year after year without you doing a thing. However, an increase in the value of your house won't change your life. You've still got to live in it, whatever it may be worth, and you've still got to go to work to pay the mortgage. The market goes up and, as they say, a rising tide lifts all boats, but this book will show you a formula that will make money from property even in a falling market. My twelve-week property plan will enable you to eventually give up the day job, if that's your goal, become your own boss and achieve mastery of your destiny. It could really prove the very next best thing to winning the lottery. But, is this prospect genuinely available to YOU? Or, does success in this field require skills, knowledge, luck, cunning, capital and connections that you'll never be able to acquire?

The answer is, if you really want to make money from property, you CAN, and in fact this may be one of the best times to do so. You can start from nothing like I did, and it doesn't matter what kind of education you've had, whether you've got anything in the bank or where you live. You don't need a special kind of intelligence, insider tips or the ability to predict market movements. It is not rocket science; you just need to understand the formula and that is what I am going to share with you.

Surely you can only make money in a rising market? Whenever a market's rising, people will be predicting grimly that it's about to fall. Yet, the people who've made fortunes in any field have rarely done so by anticipating market movements. No one can do that consistently; many of the world's billionaires have made fortunes in a falling market. The fact is, however, that you can make money out of property in a falling market, as well as in a rising one. In some ways, it's easier to do so for the simple reason that people start to get nervous then panic, and when people panic, that's the time when you can pick up a bargain!

If you still think you've got to be specially blessed to succeed, let me tell you my own story. I grew up on a council estate in Northern Ireland during the Troubles. I was the oldest of seven children, and my awesome mum, Kathleen, was 19 when I was born. My dad, Dessie, was an engineer and always provided for us through the hard times. I spent weeks in hospital with severe asthma, but by the time I was seven or eight, the idea of owning and being involved in property had begun to fascinate me.

I failed the 11-plus (which we still have in Northern Ireland), but that wasn't going to stop me, and with my interest in buildings, I got myself work experience at a local architect's practice. One day, this cool, immaculately suited guy drove up to the office in a silver Porsche – rarely seen in Northern Ireland in those days. Confidently, he spelt out an elaborate array of requirements for a new scheme we were working on, buildings, fittings, landscaping and much more besides, while the architects I'd looked up to dutifully noted his every word. When he'd gone, I asked who he was. 'He is the client. He is the property developer,' I was told. I realised that's what I wanted to do someday, I wanted to be the person making it happen.

I then studied and planned my career – doing a four-year degree course in Estate Management, and then a post-graduate diploma in accountancy because I thought it would be useful in property to understand the figures. But the property market had crashed in the early 90s, and I ended up as an accountant counting sausages in a factory. Within a year I thankfully got out of that and landed a job as a property manager for a telecoms firm. I was back in property where I belonged and worked hard and moved up the corporate ladder rapidly, getting over ten years of invaluable property experience under my belt. Although I bought, sold and managed literally billions of pounds and property, office life was full of frustrations and glass ceilings that stopped my growth and ambitions. I still wanted to be my own boss. So, at the age of 33, I took the biggest risk of my life, walked out of my high-flying job and set up my own property business.

Using my savings, I started doing up one-bedroom flats, but to go further, I needed more money, but the banks wouldn't give me any. I found a business partner, a builder to take me to the next level. For lots of reasons this was a challenging partnership, but it got me up and running. Then, I eventually bought and converted a house into six luxury apartments, making enough profit to really get started. Within about three years, I'd made my first million (on paper at least), and since then my business has continued to grow at a phenomenal rate. Currently, I'm looking at schemes of several hundred units, involving tens of millions of pounds, buying hotels, building apartments abroad and developing my TV and media business.

I love every minute spent on property development. I live, eat and breathe property. Now I want to share some of the knowledge with you. When I tell people that it is possible to make a million, I remind them that the million is a metaphor for reaching your goals. Money, in itself, is not everything in life – family and friends are much more important – but making money from property will give you the freedom to have the life you want. I started sharing my expertise by presenting property programmes on Channel Five. I appear regularly on Sky, BBC 1 and Five TV news as a property expert and give seminars to people who want to get into the business. Now, I've written this book. It will tell you the ins and outs you need to know to make a success of your own property portfolio.

> **As with most things in life, if you're going to succeed, you're going to have to apply yourself ruthlessly to the task**

So, is that really all there is to it? All you have to do to become a property entrepreneur is to read this book? Well, not quite. I said anyone CAN do it. I didn't say it would be easy. Lots of people think that property money is easy money, but they're wrong. Property is a tough business that needs stamina, tenacity, courage, faith and hard work. I have had many dark hours when my business seemed to be falling apart, but I have held the business together and bounced back. You will have to do things that don't necessarily come naturally. And, you will have to do them with vigour, determination and panache.

When you start, you will find that the odds seem stacked against you. Nothing will be handed to you on a silver platter. People will not believe in you. When you ask them to lend you money, they may laugh in your face. Vital sales will fall through on the day you are supposed to be exchanging contracts. Business partners will let you down. You will have to develop the psychological armour to deal with all this. You will have to nurture the self-belief that will enable you to impose your will on events.

If you don't like the sound of that, now is the time to recognise that property is not for you. Having read this book you can make an informed choice, about whether you want to become a property success or not. It is entirely up to you. So stiffen your sinews and pluck up your courage. And now read on. Let me show you how to make your first million. Let's make it happen for you...

Life-changing deals

...it only takes one deal to change your life!

What is a life-changing deal? A life-changing deal will allow you to take financial control of your destiny. It will give you independence, and offer choices and alternatives. In short it will give you the opportunity to change your life on your terms. I consider a life-changing deal as one that makes a profit of up to £50,000. Although this seems like a huge amount of money, in property development terms it is a reasonable starting point. This is the beginning of your road to making money from property and all you have to do is find a deal to give you the capital to change how you live your life. And that's exactly what I'm going to show you how to do, but the first question is how to establish whether a deal is life changing or not?

Imagine moving into the diamond business. The first thing diamond experts will do is find a site that they know has diamonds – and to do that they put vast amounts of time into researching that location. There is no point in digging for diamonds in the wrong area! Now, diamonds come in lots of different qualities, shapes and forms and not only do you need to know where to look, you also need to know what you are looking for. You have got to appreciate the clarity, colour, carat and ultimately the cut. These four things all have to be at a very high level to make the diamond valuable. All the boxes must be ticked and obviously the more experienced the diamond expert is, the more chance he has of spotting that incredibly flawless stone. So faced with a seemingly worthless piece of rock, an experienced diamond expert will crack it open and find a priceless gem. Like the diamond expert, you are looking for a diamond in the rough.

It's buying that makes the difference

Get your life-changing deal right, and it can change your life. Like magic, these deals can sweep you out of your day job, and allow you to create a business of your own that will give you the financial independence that you've always craved. They can cast a spell over your life, leaving you the master of your own destiny, instead of a slave to the ambitions of others. They can be the genie that empowers you to achieve whatever you want.

Most businesses are built on a whole raft of deal-making. The beauty of property is that just one great deal at the very beginning can thrust you straight into the ranks of the serious players. Your first purchase can end up yielding the tens of thousands of pounds that will snowball through successive deals. Beyond that, if you want to go that far, you can find yourself making hundreds of thousands of pounds or even millions from a single deal.

Now I'm going to teach you the key elements that you need to know to find your life-changing deal. No deal will score 100 per cent on all of them. But, you should be looking for the opportunities that offer a good showing on as many of them as possible. Remember, a life-changing deal must have five essential elements:

1. Price. At least 20 per cent below the market value, now more like 25 per cent (unless you can add value to the property, which you will find out how to do in chapter 11)
2. Location. The peripheral area that's going up
3. Market. Know who is going to buy your property (local know-how not global trends)
4. Adding value. Find a wreck (the worst house in the best street)
5. Timing. Time is money (always have an exit strategy)

> **It's the quality of the initial deal that really matters more than anything else**

Your life-changing deal must have these five essential elements and if one of these is missing your deal may be worthless. Let's get one thing clear from the outset. Maybe you'll succeed in boosting the value of your properties through loving renovation and cunning improvements. Maybe (with the help of this book) you'll prove a wizard at calculating how and when to sell. Yet your efforts in these fields are most unlikely to do the trick if you get it wrong at square one, especially in today's world.

1 Price

It's surprising how many people make mistakes in life by overlooking the blindingly obvious. Not you, of course. I'm sure you already appreciate that the price at which you buy is pretty important. Well, you're even more right than you thought you were. It's when you buy that you can choose where to put your money. When you sell, you've got no such room for manoeuvre. You're much more likely to be at the mercy of the marketplace. Think about it, it's when you buy, not when you sell, that you can expect to make your money. Understand this point; it is the crux to making your first million.

Twenty-five per cent less than market value
What, though, is a good price? It's not some figure that doesn't seem too bad when a property has taken your liking. You've got to take a much harsher attitude. Essentially, you must be certain

before you make a move that what you're going to pay is substantially less than the real market value. How much is substantially? At least 25 per cent. And, you've got to be sure that you're really hitting this target, not by guessing, but by checking the prices that comparable properties in the same street are actually fetching. It's absolutely essential that you get a bargain. There is, however, a caveat to this rule – you may pay the full asking price to take a property off the market quickly when you know you can add incredible value to the property through planning permission or refurbishment.

Motivated sellers

Who, though, is going to sell you a house for less than it's worth? Well, there's always someone, and with the credit crunch there are now thousands of opportunities everywhere. People we can call motivated sellers. For some reason or other, they are not going to hold out for the true value of their home. Maybe they have to move abroad quickly. Maybe she's getting a divorce and wants her share of the cash fast. Maybe his health problems require an instant move. Somebody who's lost a job may be keen to sell up before repossession hits. These are your motivated sellers, and the more motivated they are, the better for you. Their motivation becomes your discount.

For example, builders coming out of developments always have one or two flats that they struggle to sell, maybe because these are awkwardly shaped or offer a view of the waste bins. Developers need to cash in and move on, especially if they're burdened by debt. Often, they'll take whatever they can get for their last few units. If you come in with a fast and aggressive offer, you can do very well with what we might call the last-minute pounce.

> " Find out why the seller is selling. The more you get to understand their situation, the more effectively you'll be able to strike a great deal "

Sometimes the motivation for a quick sale is quite unusual. I once came across a seller who had been the mistress of a rich banker. She had inherited a house from him, but he had left everything else to his widow and their three daughters. The family wanted the house as well, and they were contesting the will. The ex-mistress was advised that if she sold the property quickly enough, she could vastly complicate the family's legal challenge. She didn't want to advertise the house for fear of alerting them. A tough situation for her, but a purchase for me at much less than market value. Such are the many guises in which motivated buyers appear. Your job is to spot them and swoop on them fast. Remember, this is a business transaction, not an emotional commitment.

Search for the deal

Clearly, you're going to have to develop an inquisitive mind set. Whenever I'm looking at property, I knock on neighbours' doors and ask a lot of questions. If I go into an estate agent's, I ask who on their books is most eager to sell. And, once I've got to a seller, I bombard him or her with questions. Why do you want to sell? How long has your house been on the market? Can you afford to wait much longer? What about a lower price for a quick sale?

Perhaps you're the shy type, and you don't like the sound of any of this. Put this book down now. You've wasted your money. Try and find another way to get rich. Striking the life-changing deal requires tough psychological gamesmanship. You can't play the game an easy way, by writing letters or sending emails. You've got to see the whites of people's eyes, and go for it.

Once you start living and breathing the search for the life-changing deal that you can get at the right price, you may start to grow into a different kind of person. The quest can become totally absorbing. The process is essentially simple, but it requires total commitment. Rest assured, however, that the effort involved is going to pay off. All business is about buying cheap and selling dear. But in the property game, it's the buying that matters so much more than the selling. It is all about the price you pay. Remember, you are in control of the buying and not of the selling.

2 Location

Location in my mind is the second most important factor to finding a life-changing deal. Property-seekers are often offered a supposedly hot tip by those who think they're in the know. If you haven't yet heard this mantra, you certainly will – 'There are only three things that matter when it comes to choosing property:

location, location, and location.' It's not entirely true. You already know there are five crucial factors, not just one. Nonetheless, the whereabouts of your property is only the second most important decision you'll make, because if you buy at the right price you can still make a profit in a seemingly bad location. So as far as I am concerned, location is not as important as price.

Places with potential

All the same, you need to be clear exactly what this means. The word 'location' can lead you astray. For lots of people, it means the best part of town, the fanciest area. That's not what you're after at all. Often, the poshest places have already realised most of their potential. Prices there may be high, but they're not necessarily going to rise in future as fast as they will elsewhere. What you want is a headroom area, which is cheap now, but clearly on the up-and-up. Here, not only may prices rise faster, but also you are more likely to find opportunities to add value, since there'll be more property that hasn't already been renovated. Make sure you have a clinical approach to the price you intend to pay.

Skip streets

Look out for skips on the road. Their presence means people are already starting to invest in the area. Often such places are close to, but not inside, the highest-priced parts of town. People who can't afford to live where they'd really like to often settle instead for what's next door.

A year or so after a street fills up with skips, take a look at the next street on the side that's further out. You may well find it filling up with skips of its own. Then the next street will follow, as a ripple effect builds up. You can find this process producing houses 40 per cent cheaper than their counterparts just one street away, if they've yet to be touched by gentrification. Your job is to sniff out the places where this is happening. Start with the most highly desirable areas where the postcodes are fashionable and add a premium to the price, and work your way outwards until you find the skips.

When you've found a place with skip streets, look out for other indicators of upward mobility. Are supermarket chains and wine shops opening? Are estate agents moving in, especially the big chains? Have major banks got branches in the high street? Boutique businesses, like art galleries, delicatessens, cafés and fashion shops, are reliable giveaways. New blocks of flats and office buildings are reassuring, especially if big companies are moving in.

Places with transport

Get ahead of the curve by finding out about planned transport links that have yet to materialise and regeneration schemes that are still on the drawing board. Go into the town hall and ask to see the 'UDP', or Unitary Development Plan, which will tell you what's coming up. Ask if a major employer is about to move in. In London, planned Tube extensions have proved a goldmine for some. I have friends who bought in Bermondsey before the Jubilee Line extension opened. Once it did, prices went through the roof, yet the plan for the new station had existed for years. My friends had spotted a case of 'planning pregnancy'.

In his book, *The Art of the Deal*, the great American property dealer Donald Trump says he doesn't find locations, he creates them. I decided to try and achieve the same thing. When I did my first development in the vicinity of Richmond Hill in London, the place I chose wasn't called 'Richmond Hill', but 'The Alberts'. It was home to the workers who serviced Richmond's rich in Victorian times. Still, it was on the brow of Richmond Hill, so I advertised my property as 'The Alberts, Richmond Hill'. The local estate agents told me I wouldn't get away with this. Well, the development is now called 'The Alberts, Richmond Hill'. It looks great, the location is fantastic, and everybody thinks of it as being in Richmond Hill. Single-handedly, I enlarged Richmond Hill. In due course, you could pull off the same kind of trick.

It's often easy to piggyback on the reputation of a glamorous and charismatic area. Battersea, just across the river from Chelsea, is sometimes called 'South Chelsea' by those seeking to sell property to would-be Sloanes of limited means. People not strictly within Chelsea's bounds will happily call their shop the 'Chelsea Boutique'. Developments calling themselves something like 'Chelsea Riverside' or the 'Chelsea Apartments' sprawl ever further round the area's perimeter. Before you know it, Chelsea has got much bigger, and all the property owners in the new periphery can cash in.

Places with public amenities

Just as you've got to seek out the motivated seller, so you've got to get inside the minds of your own potential buyers. Will they care about decent public transport and parks? If your property has no parking or outside space, then they probably will. If it has a double garage and a luxurious garden, then they probably won't. A horrible view may not matter in a buy-to-let that will have a high turnover of busy tenants. It could ruin the sale prospects of an otherwise charming house of character.

Education

If your target market is families, think about schooling prospects. In cities where education is a problem, prices in the catchment areas of well-regarded schools can soar above those in otherwise comparable districts. If your property's aimed at yuppie singles and couples, this may not be an issue at all. If it's a family home, it may matter more than anything else. If this is the case, you've got lots of research to do. Get talking to people in the local community. Word of mouth will tell you more than test results or league table rankings.

3 Market

You now understand the importance or price and location. The next vital question is, who is the target market and will they buy or rent this property? You also have to be aware of the overall market as a whole. The question I'm asked more often than any other is, 'Will the market crash?'. Well, we have certainly seen a correction and at the time of updating this book prices have fallen by nearly 20 per cent!

Is the market crashing?

Prophets of doom in the housing market have been growing more vociferous for a long time. In other markets, most obviously America, prices have indeed turned down. And now, thanks to the credit crunch, they are falling in the UK as well. Should you therefore abandon your ambition to make money? NO! If anything, in a falling market there are more opportunities. The reason? The number of motivated sellers increases

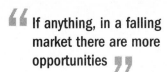

If anything, in a falling market there are more opportunities

dramatically, they want to downsize or offload and sell up, either way there's a huge amount of opportunities.

Market economics

To understand why this is so, you need to get a firm grip on certain realities. Property is quite different from most other assets. To exist, human beings need three things: water, food and shelter. Demand for these things is never going to disappear as long as our species survives. The thirst for a piece of territory is one of the most powerful of human drives. A passion for home and hearth drives people to work their fingers to the bone and to fight wars. Getting the living space we want defines our identities and creates the security we need to get on with our lives. That's why people become so emotional about their homes. That's why they always desire houses, and why some of them will always want bigger and better ones.

The same sentiments underpin the rise in property prices that's taken place over the last decade. Look at the graph below. It shows the price of the average house rising in real terms from around £70,000 in 1995 to around £186,000 at the beginning of 2008. But this has changed – at the time of writing, in late 2008, it has fallen back to around £158,000. Will it continue to drop?

Nobody knows for sure, but if a property market is to remain vigorous, several key conditions have to be met. You need low

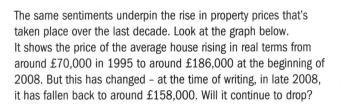

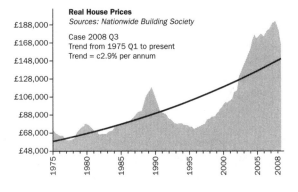

Real House Prices
Sources: Nationwide Building Society

Case 2008 Q3
Trend from 1975 Q1 to present
Trend = c2.9% per annum

unemployment, low inflation, an excess of demand, an optimistic public mood, and of course, importantly, low interest rates.

Interest rates

In the short term, it's interest rates that have the most immediate impact. These rates determine how much mortgages cost. The lower they are, the more people can borrow, and the more housing they can therefore buy. As inflation fell in the 1990s, interest rates came down too, and more people were able to fulfil their desire for homes of their own. The Government has an inflation target of 2 per cent that it tries to control with what is known as monetary policy – the Bank of England adjusts the money supply via interest rates. To manage the current economic slowdown, the Bank of England are again lowering interest rates. Look at my next graph. It shows interest rates increasing from 3.5 per cent in 2003 to 5.75 per cent in 2007– although it dropped to 5.5 per cent in January 2008 and is now back to 3 per cent. And I expect them to go down to 2 per cent in 2009, which certainly should stabilise the current downturn.

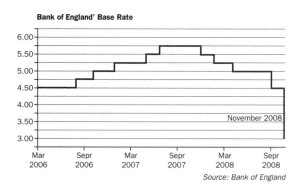

Bank of England' Base Rate

Source: Bank of England

Changing interest rates pose the biggest immediate threat to property prices. Some people who might otherwise have taken out mortgages find they can no longer afford to. Some of those who already have mortgages enjoy interest rates pegged for a fixed term. When these terms expire, they will suddenly have to switch to higher, variable rates. Some may find they can no longer make their repayments. If their homes are repossessed, these could flood the market and depress prices. The bottom line is, the lower the interest rate, the easier it is for people to afford to buy property, hence demand and prices usually go up.

American issues

That's the spectre. All the same, Britain isn't like the United States. It's not just that we've had less lending to people likely to default on their mortgages; there's something much more fundamental. In America there's a lot more space, and a lot less planning control. As a result American developers have built more houses in some areas than there are people to live in them. In Britain, on the whole there's shortage of homes, and planning restrictions mean there's not much land on which to build more. However, there are places in the UK where an extremely overheated market has led to over-supply in some places like Manchester, Leeds and Belfast, but these are exceptions and should balance out over time.

First-time buyers

There are other things we could worry ourselves about. Look at my next graph. It shows the percentage of first-time buyers in the marketplace. They've fallen from 55 per cent of house purchasers in 1993 to 38 per cent in 2003, and this continues to fall. Why should that matter? Well, it's first-time buyers who drive the whole of the housing market. They fire up the bottom tier, and then push the rest of the system forwards as they move ever onwards and upwards. When they fall away, the whole market weakens.

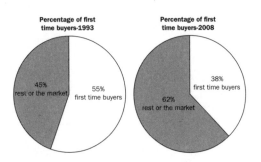

Percentage of first time buyers-1993

45% rest or the market
55% first time buyers

Percentage of first time buyers-2008

38% first time buyers
62% rest or the market

As property prices have risen, young people have found that the prices of what would have been starter homes have soared way out of their reach. This is because such property has fallen into the hands of people who can afford to buy additional homes and rent these out to others. This process could lead to more and more people spending their whole lives in rented property, and so the home ownership market drops.

Such, then, are the threats to the continuing property-price boom. The economy has started to struggle and we are in a recession, nationally and globally.

Cyclical downturn

The housing market is currently falling. If it continues to fall, should you give up your quest for a property empire? Well, the answer's still no. For the reasons I've indicated, and even with the current global downturn, any property-price fall in Britain or Ireland would be no more than a cyclical downturn in a long-term trend that can only go upward. Any kind of investor in any market has to recognise that prices can sometimes go down as well as up. Wise investors recognise they must accept this. For the short-term, movements of markets are beyond anyone's control. The idea that you can avoid turbulence by guessing the timing of market fluctuations is an illusion. You must take a long-term view.

If investors in the mid-1990s hadn't bought property, they would have lost out on huge amounts of money. Investors who listened to the doom and gloom merchants then would have missed out on the massive gains that followed. Yet, that doesn't mean that these Jeremiahs aren't going to be proved right in the end.

Market downturn opportunities

At almost any time, there's a case for staying out of any market because things might go wrong. Yet, if you stay on the quayside, you certainly won't make money. If you dive in, you may hit a patch of choppy water, but you should still have a productive swim if you know where you're heading. You need to decide now; do you want to be a spectator or a competitive player?

> **If you stay on the quayside, you certainly won't make money**

Of course, a market downturn is an opportunity as well as a challenge. If you go in at the bottom, you'll rise that much further when the market recovers its vim and gusto. Yet, that doesn't mean you should wait for what you think may be a trough. An apparently depressed market may fall yet further. Or, while you're waiting for it to fall, it may scale further heights. If it does, you won't be getting the benefit.

The key to successful investment in property, as in any other asset, doesn't lie in trying to second-guess market timing, but in getting the fundamentals right. If you do that, and the market drops by 20 per cent, you should still be okay. The house that you bought cheap, in a good location, may lose some value, but you can still sell and get out with the shirt on your back. However, if you hang on in, it will go up again eventually. The logic of the property market is that in the long-term prices will rise, because people want houses and people get richer.

Of course, you should keep an eye on the overall housing market. If you like, you can also follow the progress of the global economy. You can try to guess how its ups and downs might feed into British interest rates. Your guesses may be as good as anyone else's. The key element to remember is what Mark Twain said in the 19th century, 'The thing about land is they are not making any more of it.'

> ** The thing about land is they are not making any more of it **

Right now things are tough, but over the long term property prices will rise, that's a fact. It's simple supply versus demand.

Micro-market

It's up to you to choose whether to expend effort on watching the macro-market (the big picture). Yet, whatever you decide on this point, there's a completely different kind of market to which you MUST pay close attention. This arena is very different from the global stage that plays host to the forces of economic history. It's the local property micro-market in which you'll actually be doing your business. The dynamics of the communities in which you actually buy and sell may give a potential deal that vital injection of magic. At certain moments, the workings of your micro-market may well be overshadowed by events in the wider world in which it's suspended. But, it's on what happens close at hand, not outside influences, that you must concentrate if you're going to make that million.

Instead of perusing the *Wall Street Journal*, prowl the streets of your own locality and sniff the air. Read local newspapers, scour the Internet for local blogs, talk to property developers, grill shopkeepers, and pester your friends and your acquaintances. Are estate agents being swamped by people looking for property? Or, have their calls dried up? Are their shop-windows filled with pictures of the same houses week after week? Or, are they so busy that houses are disappearing before their particulars even get printed? The answers to all these questions can help determine whether a deal is sweet or not.

" The more motivated your buyers, the more they will pay you ""

Motivated buyers

This is the point where you need to consider who you are going to sell your property to. Your impressions may be worth much more than formal statistics, which inevitably lag what's happening on the ground. By building your own picture of one locality, you can get to know more about it than anyone else. You need to study the character of your potential buyer just as you need to study that of a potential seller. And, just as you have to find the motivated seller, so you should check out whether the motivated buyer is readily on hand. You already know that the more motivated your sellers, the less you need to pay them. Well, the more motivated your buyers, the more they will pay you. Inversely, the opposite is also true.

Concentrate on the profile of potential purchasers within your area. How many are professionals, students, first-time buyers, families, divorcees, blue-collar workers, immigrants, retired people, buy-to-let investors? How are these proportions changing week by week? How eager to buy is each of the different groups? On what does their eagerness depend? Write down the criteria that your buyer will have. Make a list of the top five things they will look for.

Super-rich buyers

If your area attracts City traders flush with huge Christmas bonuses (if there are any left!), you may find them as putty in your hands. Hard-pressed family buyers, on the other hand, will drive a harder bargain. Are there any mega-buyers in your area that will pay virtually any price for a property that exactly meets their particular requirements? How are the requirements of the super-rich changing? Are second bathrooms becoming essential? Do people like loft conversions? Are conservatories seen as must-have or a bit of a bore?

Studying such matters will help you determine whether the property you're thinking of buying is the right one or not. Will it appeal to the kind of people who are looking for homes in the area? If not, you won't be able to get it off your hands at a decent price, whatever's happening to the national or the international market. You could even find yourself stuck with something you can't shift at all – that would really push your profit into the middle distance. On the other hand, a good house or flat in an area where people want the kind of property you'll be offering should sell for a price, even during a downturn, and that will at least keep you in the game.

Analysing the make-up of local life may seem more mundane than trying to interpret the grand sweep of the big picture. Yet, it's the state of the market under your nose that matters when you're assessing that crucial deal.

4 Adding value

Now that you understand the importance of price, location and your target market, the next crucial aspect to consider is how to add value to your property.

What looks like a clever purchase price may turn out to be less clever than you think. Moreover, while the wider market may be booming when you buy, it can also fall, sometimes quite suddenly, as we've seen recently. When that happens, traders relying simply on being able to buy low and sell high tend to get caught out.

The only way you can be sure of making a substantial sum out of each of your projects is by making it worth more than it would otherwise fetch. And, you'll only be able to do that if the property you buy offers scope for improvement. If it does, you stand to make big gains, even if property prices are generally falling.

> **Ideally, you want to create the most valued property of its kind in the area...**

So the more scope there is, the better your prospects are. The more value you can add to your property, the more profit you usually get on your bottom line.

Find a wreck

So, a perfect property, elegantly proportioned, with the right number of bathrooms, tastefully decorated in neutral colours, with a loft conversion already in place, a splendid conservatory and the latest flooring, may be the last thing you want. You're after an ugly, misshapen, down-at-heel dump, if not a complete wreck. Nonetheless, you have to be able to see exactly how you're going to turn it into something eminently desirable. Remember – you are looking for a diamond in the rough. You want to be able to add value.

This means that BEFORE, not AFTER, you close your deal, you've got to discover exactly what opportunities will be available. Ideally, you want to create the most valued property of its kind in the area in which you're operating. If you can't manage that, you want to get as close to this as possible. Try to find the worst house in the best street, with a view to turning it into the best house in that street. Never buy the best house in the worst street because that is making life difficult, if not impossible, to turn a profit. Root around among those skip streets we talked about, and find a house that doesn't yet have its skip but stands greatly in need of one.

Adding lofts, kitchens and bathrooms

Adding value may mean going into the loft, building a conservatory, adding an extension or reconforming rooms to create more bathrooms or a better kitchen. It may mean simply refurbishing an existing set-up by rewiring, removing off-putting decoration, replacing kitchen and bathroom fittings and perhaps restoring original features. It could mean turning a basement into a granny flat, or even building a new home at the end of a large garden.

On a basic level, opening up a kitchen and making an extra bedroom are often the most profitable moves. Sometimes you can produce an extra room by moving the kitchen into the living room and creating an open-plan space that a buyer may actually prefer. A one-bedroom flat can become a two-bedder, if you can convert a dining room. This move alone could add on average, tens of thousands to the property's value, as a two-bedroom flat is worth more than a one-bedroom flat.

As the developer, you must always add value to your properties. If the market falls, you will still get equity return. It is important to know which renovations will add value and which ones won't give you a return. I consider in the following to be the most effective:

Build an extension. Extending your property is an ambitious and expensive move. Any significant building work will cause disruption and reduce outdoor space. On the other hand, extra square footage can be a real advantage. Make sure your plans are in line with the style of your property (especially in period homes), and that the extension will add functional living space. It's not wise, for example, to add bedrooms when you have a living room the size of a postage stamp. Another common mistake is tacking on a half-hearted conservatory without choosing the most suitable design or making efforts to define usage.

> " You must always add value to your properties. If the market falls, you will still get equity return "

Convert the loft or cellar. Most home improvements will add some value, but the cleverest will reap rewards in relation to outlay. According to valuers in the Halifax Home Improvement Survey 2006, loft conversions represent the best value for money. Prices start at around £8,000 and most lofts with a roof height of at least 2.4 metres are suitable for conversion. Loft conversions are normally used to add another bedroom, and there's often space for a value-boosting en-suite.

Some people will try basement conversions – this is not for the faint-hearted. It is structurally complicated, and costs several times more that a loft conversion, making it risky for profit margins. Extensions, loft and basement conversions involve major building work and require expert help.

Add extra bedrooms. Whether you extend or convert existing space, it's tempting to add an extra bedroom. This has a satisfyingly visible effect on estate agents' statistics. Figures released by Nationwide in 2003 showed that adding a bedroom could increase value by 11 per cent.

It's wise to consider the proportions of your home and avoid cramming in additional bedrooms unnecessarily. Think about your potential market. Families may want to give children small rooms of their own, but couples or single-occupiers often prefer one or two spacious bedrooms.

Open up space. There's no sign that the trend for open-plan living is going away. And why should it? Many people find it family-friendly, and good for entertaining. Just don't get carried away. Practical family homes often need rooms to shut away white goods, household waste and pets, and to separate adults and children. It's also essential to get the professionals in to make sure you're not bashing down load-bearing walls.

" **Kitchen-diners are a popular use of space, but the sitting room is still considered the most important room in the house** "

The most successful open-plan rooms tend to be 'zoned' to define space. Make it clear which area could fit a dining table, and where a desk can go, for example.

Install central heating. Fitting central heating is not the most inspiring project, but it's a must-do for anyone renovating a property without it. While other improvements have the potential to go wrong, central heating and a modern boiler are a safe bet.

Figures from Nationwide suggest this can add 13 per cent to the value of a property.

Even if your property already has central heating, investment in a new, high-efficiency boiler is worth considering. These can cost £100–£200 more than conventional boilers, but will reduce heating bills and attract 'green' buyers.

Re-fit the kitchen. Kitchens suffer serious wear and tear during their lifetime, and a new one can add real 'wow' factor to a property. Valuers in the Halifax survey placed a modern fitted kitchen second (after a loft conversion) in their list of home improvements most likely to add value. Again, it's important to think things through and weigh up the cost of improvement against the overall value of the property. Buyers often judge a property on the appearance of the kitchen.

> " Having a 'cool' bathroom helps sell your property faster and for more money "

Beware of over-spending, you can easily spend tens of thousands on a top-of-the-range kitchen, but somewhere between £3,000 and £15,000 is usually sufficient – depending on your market.

Update the bathroom. Like kitchens, bathrooms can quickly look shabby and dated. A new one could set you back thousands, but it's possible to get a decent suite for around £500 – again, depending on your market.

If you're competing with newer properties in your area, consider adding, or re-arranging rooms to increase the bathroom-to-bedroom ratio. These days, even small properties tend to be built with an en-suite leading from the master bedroom in addition to a main bathroom. When it comes to increasing the value of your property, research has shown that adding an extra bathroom adds about 10 per cent to a home's value. In some areas, such as London, this rose to over 15 per cent! And in my experience, having a 'cool' bathroom helps sell your property faster and for more money.

Bear in mind that the key to maximising the value you get from an en-suite is to make sure that you do the job well – particularly if you live in an urban area where the housing market is competitive. It certainly requires a toilet, hand basin and shower, at the very minimum, with a bath somewhere else in the property.

> **Simply by filling in a form and securing bureaucratic approval, you can increase a property's value overnight**

Be realistic, though. Is there enough room to add an en-suite? If you lose too much bedroom space – so a double bed no longer fits, for example – it may not be worth doing. And will you bump your head when you climb into the shower? Check the position of your existing water and waste pipes, too – how easy will it be to connect these up to your new bathroom? If you are not sure, get a reliable plumber to give you some advice. Will the en-suite have a window? If not, could you fit a dormer or Velux window to bring light and ventilation in?

Get planning permission. Some operations may require no more than a trip to the hardware store. Yet almost any major work will bring you up against one crucial feature of adding value: planning permission. Here, a kind of magic is genuinely at work. In some cases, simply by filling in a form and securing bureaucratic approval, you can increase a property's value overnight.

This may be true even if you don't bother to carry out the work that you've proposed. Just by selling property after securing permission for development, you can make serious money. Some people have become billionaires simply by exploiting the planning system. You can pick up an acre of farmland for a few thousand pounds. If it's in the right place, and you can get planning permission to build executive housing on the site, you could sell that same acre for a couple of million, without bothering to lay a brick.

That's the kind of thing you may eventually get up to, when you're further down the road. At the outset on smaller scale projects you'll do best if you actually carry out the work for which you've secured permission. It's particularly worthwhile to make such efforts here in Britain, because, as we've seen, there's a shortage of property. Many people would like a decent family home with a big kitchen and a couple of bathrooms. Such homes may not be easy to find in the places in which they want to live. But you may be able to create one for them out of a much less spacious property. Your micro-market research should have told you whether this is the way forward, or whether instead you should be carving out granny flats or home offices.

However, to add value, and perform any kind of substantial value operation, you'll actually have to get that planning permission. This means that BEFORE you cut your deal, you're going to have to find out what will be allowed. So, you'll have to plunge yourself into the antiquated, subjective and often bizarre world of the planning system. Then, you'll have to discover how likely it is that your particular scheme will actually win approval.

That means hitting the planning textbooks. It means many trips to the town hall to talk to officials about the lie of the land in your particular area, about bureaucratic policy, and about the attitudes of local politicians. Ask to see planning applications made by householders in the road that interests you. Often, council staff are surprisingly helpful. Far fewer people bother them with these essential questions than you might expect.

At the same time you need to look around. If the street you're interested in already has lots of loft extensions, you can probably have one as well. If, however, no one's gone beyond the roof-line, this may not be allowed. Similarly, if there are plenty of new back additions, you too can probably expand. If front gardens have been paved for car parking, perhaps you can pave yours as well. Talk to neighbouring owners about their experiences. Not just about what they've managed to do, but about what has been forbidden.

> " **Consider permitted development. It allows you to do a certain amount of rearrangement of your property without any special permission** "

What, though, if all this diligent research produces unwelcome news? Suppose the local council is firmly opposed to all home expansion. It may be worried about the generation of extra traffic or the destruction of local character. The more attractive the area, the tougher the line it is likely to take. In conservation areas, you may find you can't do much at all. If your target property is listed as a historic building, you'll need special permission to do anything serious, and you're highly likely to be turned down. All the same, you shouldn't despair.

You can consider permitted development. It allows you to do a certain amount of rearrangement of your property without any special permission. Essentially, you can increase the square footage of most properties by a certain percentage without asking anyone. This provision often covers things like loft extensions and conservatories, as well as much internal work. In some of these cases, you may still have to conform to building controls, but these exist simply to ensure that the work you do is safe.

5 Timing

As you're now well aware, timing your purchase to make the most of fluctuations in the global property market is NOT the way to make a life-changing deal. Yet, timing of another kind is indeed an important factor. Once again, it's your immediate circumstances that you need to take account of.

Will the seller's circumstances allow you to complete the purchase by the time you need to? Sometimes someone wants to stay in the house he's selling for a considerable time to come. Maybe he's moving to a new job the following year. It's very sensible of him to fix up his house sale ahead of time, if he can manage to do so. But it may not be sensible for you to freeze your own activities while you wait for him to vacate.

Can you get your own funding together quickly enough? Are you borrowing from an institution that's going to take its time over surveys and credit checks? If so, a cash buyer could sneak in under your nose and set your efforts at nought. Exploring prospects in-depth, long before you'll be ready to act, could just be a waste of time.

Creating a timetable

This is the time to start your schedule. You may need to find out the likely length of a wait for planning permission. You may find you can't afford the time to tangle with planners at all. You'll have to schedule all of the building works you intend to undertake. Otherwise, you won't know when you'll be ready to bring your property to market.

If you don't know when your sale will happen, how can you be sure you'll have enough money to tide you over the gap? How will you know that the purchasers that you'll need will actually be around? How will you ensure you'll have the money you're going to require to make your next purchase possible? To answer these questions, you're going to have to timetable all the activities that make up your project. Look at the twelve-week property plan starting on page 179.

Time is money in property development, especially if you're borrowing large sums. You may find yourself making interest payments on a scale you'd otherwise find unimaginable. Many of the factors on which you'll depend are subject to rapid change. Interest rates can rise, and so can building costs. Or, builders may suddenly become much harder to find. This is particularly likely to happen if you've selected an area in which many other houses are being refurbished. And, of course, if this isn't happening, you've probably chosen the wrong area.

For these, and other reasons, you'll nearly always want a rapid turnaround. The faster you can complete the cycle of buying, improving and selling, the more quickly you'll achieve your goals. Does the deal you're looking at fit the timetable you require? Remember that while you tie yourself up in one protracted venture, you're using up time that could be spent on projects you could turn around more quickly.

Refurbishment may add value, but it takes time. The more time it takes, the more it will sap the real value of whatever profit you eventually make. You, therefore, need to assess whether the improvements you'd have to make could be completed quickly enough to meet the requirements of your venture.

Selling

You should look at the sales process as well. Some properties in some marketplaces will go like hot cakes. Others, particularly more unusual, non-standard properties, can take much longer to shift. You may be convinced that such a property is worth a high price, particularly if you've put a lot of effort into refurbishing it – and, so it will be, if and when it finds a buyer who shares your enthusiasm for it. However, if this could take a long time to happen, you need to factor this consideration into your calculations.

Closing the deal

At the same time, you can't afford to spend too much time weighing up risks before you make a purchase. If a prospect is as good as it ought to be in order to attract your interest, other people will also spot its potential. While you're reflecting, they can snatch it from under your nose. Once all five essential boxes have been ticked, close the deal as fast as you possibly can!

On the other hand, after you've invested effort in exploring every aspect of a possible purchase, don't be too reluctant to write off all the time you've spent on the task. Some people gradually realise that a prospective deal won't be quite as magical as they'd hoped. Instead of ruthlessly reassessing the situation, they allow the momentum they've built up to carry them onward, and they go ahead anyway. Big mistake.

No deal is life-changing just because you've spent a long time contemplating it. Once you've discovered that a prospect is not stacking up against our five criteria, be prepared to walk away. Even if it fails really badly on only one of our tests, that should be enough. Write off the time you've spent to experience, pull out, and reopen the search (I call it school fees).

Now you know all the ingredients of the life-changing deal that will form the cornerstone of your forthcoming search. You've worked out what price you want to pay, the location you want to be in, the market you're going to target, how you can add value, and what your timescales are. Now you're ready to begin looking for your deal, and this is where the hard work starts. Find that deal, and you've cracked the first and most important problem that you're going to have to face. Time, then, to relax as you sweep effortlessly onwards? Er, no. Finding a life-changing deal can be like looking for a needle in a haystack. This is where most property developers fall down, they either end up with a property that doesn't tick our five key criteria, or worse still, just give up. Most people are just lazy, if you can keep yourself motivated and keep searching, the deals are out there – now, I'm going to show you how to find them.

Finding the diamond in the rough

...there's a great property deal on virtually every street!

When I am making television shows I find it surprising how many of the contributors tell me that they 'can't find properties'. On one occasion, a couple from Liverpool argued with me until they were blue in the face, that there wasn't one deal to be found in the whole of Liverpool! Let me tell you, there are not just dozens of deals, there are not just hundreds of deals, there are thousands, if not millions, of property deals to be found in the UK alone. They're everywhere. They're next door. They're round the corner. They're in Scotland. They're in Wales. They're in England. They're in Ireland. You just need to know where to look to find your diamond in the rough.

As a young boy I used to collect golf balls from around the sides of the local golf course and then sell them back to the golfers. No point in searching for golf balls around the local tennis courts or near the local sports centre. Just like finding golf balls, or diamonds, you need to know where to look for your life-changing deal, and that's what I am going to show you. And the good news is that finding your life-changing deal is easier and much more lucrative than searching for golf balls! Here are my twelve key places to look:

1 Personal relationships: make friends and influence people

2 Auctions: wait for the hammer

3 Estate agents: they're not so bad

4 Walkabout: get on the road

5 Property finders: your little helpers

6 Newspapers and magazines: a treasure trove under your nose

7 The Internet: the way of the future

8 Public records: a cobwebby Aladdin's cave

9 The planning system: the snooper's charter

10 New developments: your shortcut to success

11 Marketing yourself: smarten up

12 Mapping systems: a bird's eye bonanza

There may be more than twelve places to look. Like everything else standing between you and property success, this task isn't easy. It isn't hard either, just so long as you remember that you'll have to apply all of the relentless effort that's also required by so many of the other aspects of your enterprise. You've got to appreciate that you're going to be looking, looking and looking, and after that, you'll be looking some more.

The search

The main reason why this bit is difficult is that yours isn't a lonely quest. A great many other people have the same idea as you. Doubtless, this book will add a few to that number. Some of them aren't as committed as you're going to have to be, and that will hold them back. All the same, even the less energetic can get lucky on occasion, and snatch your rightful prey from under your nose. More troublesome, however, will be those of your competitors, small and large, who are every bit as determined as you are. They'll quickly elbow you off the path to any life-changing deal unless you stay ruthlessly focused. And, of course, follow my wise guidance.

Rest assured, however, that the deal you need is out there. Some people tell me that in the place where they happen to be, there aren't any life-changing deals to be found. They're wrong. They aren't trying hard enough, they are not looking properly, or they're being too impatient, or possibly downright lazy. Every hour, wherever you are, whatever the state of the market, the deal you want exists. Make no mistake about it.

To understand how to find it, you have to appreciate that, essentially, you're playing a numbers game. The more properties you look at, the greater your chances of success. This isn't just a matter of mathematical logic. The more properties you see within the parameters you've established, the more you'll build up a picture of the price you should be paying, the quality of the location, your opportunities for adding value, and the character of the marketplace into which you'll eventually be selling.

> **The more properties you look at, the greater your chances of success**

Keep a record of the properties you see, and check off the extent to which they did or didn't have the makings of a life-changing deal, category by category. As you do this, you'll be building up a database in your head of the facts you need to know to identify the deal you're after. Photocopy your records and take them with you on your rounds.

Where, however, should you actually start? Should you pop round to your local estate agent? Sure, why not? You're going to have to explore every avenue you can think of. However, estate agents are just one of twelve routes that I have identified towards finding your life-changing deal that I'm going to set out, every one of which needs to be taken seriously and worked on simultaneously. You can't take them separately; you have to be working on several at a time. Use all the strategies and remember you only need to find one good deal that ticks all the boxes to get up and running.

1 Personal relationships

This is what I call 'building your wealth team'. More on this in chapter 13. The obvious roads to the deal, like the estate agent's office, can be useful, but the formal way is not the most productive in the property world. You may have heard people say, 'It's not what you know; it's who you know' – now is the time to follow this advice.

An awful lot of the deals that get done in life, the jobs that people get, and the marriage partners they end up with aren't procured through dutiful pursuit of official procedures. People pass on tips to the people they know, in the hope that the favour will one day be reciprocated. They discover that in hundreds of ways they'd never have appreciated, their own interests dovetail with those of people they bump into. What goes around, comes around. This makes networking among the most effective of all business tools. After all, deal-making is about people coming together. Without people there can be no business, so skill in managing, developing and nurturing personal relationships is a crucial asset.

Networking discriminates horribly against all those who for whatever reason are out of the loop. So, if you want to be a front-runner in the property game, you want to be among those benefiting from this unfairness, rather than losing out because of it.

Forming your team

Why do the most desirable properties in your area disappear off the market without ever appearing in an estate agent's window? Well, the very best properties often get creamed off, one way or another, behind the scenes. People who are in the know pass the word on to those whose backs they want to scratch. Kickbacks may enter into the process. But, even without immediate gain, if you can help out a mate by putting an attractive deal his or her way, would you do that, or plunge into the uncertainties of the open market?

> **The very best properties often get creamed off, one way or another, behind the scenes**

You've got to get out there, find as many potentially useful strategic partners as you can, and bond with them as closely as you can. You've got to develop the habit of seeing everybody as potentially useful, of sussing out what they may have to offer you within minutes of meeting them, of building up instant rapport, of doing favours and thereby building up credit in the favour-bank. Getting to know new people and helping them help you, is exhilarating. You're building a network, and the stronger it is the more work it will do for you.

You're listening out for someone who says she's heard that a place may be coming up for sale (when you've prompted her, of course). Somebody may turn out to have a piece of land he doesn't know what to do with. Someone else may have inherited a house she needs to get rid of. At the same time, you need to feed out messages about what you are looking for. Make special friends of any estate agent, builder, solicitor, accountant, surveyor, property developer, planner, architect, quantity surveyor, bank or building society manager you can lay your hands on. But don't forget that anybody, anywhere, in any walk of life may turn up information about a property. They all live somewhere, and so does everybody else they know.

There's no need to make this complicated. Listen, and let people know what you're up to. They'll understand, because they'd probably be doing the same thing as you if they had the time and the nerve. They may well get a vicarious thrill out of helping you on your way, but where you can make things reciprocal, do so. When my solicitors, consultants and builders bring me deals, I try and return the favour by providing them with more clients and business. Eventually, your networks ought to overlap with your network-members' networks, so that they all feed into each other for the mutual benefit of you all.

❝ Don't forget that anybody, anywhere, in any walk of life may turn up information about a property ❞

None of this takes more than business cards, an email address and a phone number. You don't need an office. Don't be afraid to be blunt and pushy; when you judge this approach is likely to be productive, then go for it. Ask that new estate agent you met at the golf club to tip you off when a hot property comes onto her books. Ask her to tell you what properties have been languishing on her books that don't deserve to. On other occasions, you may judge it right to be more subtle. Ask an architect if he knows anyone who's got planning permission but might want to sell her property. Ask anyone if they know someone who wants to move.

Knock on doors

I found the very first property I bought because someone told me about a house that looked derelict although someone seemed to live in it. I knocked on the door and asked the old man who answered if he wanted to move. He did, and my interest saved him the cost of an estate agent. Afterwards, other people who heard this story made a point of giving me similar tips.

If people can't tell you about homes for sale, they may have useful advice about what's going on in the area. They can tell you the truth about crime, parking and what the schools are really like. Strike up conversations with people in pubs and coffee shops. Be the one who dares to talk to somebody else in a bus queue. A friend of mine was told about one of his best properties by someone who was renting it, who knew it had much more potential than its owner realised.

The networking exercise

Here's an exercise you could try. Tomorrow, introduce yourself to at least five people that you don't know, either over the telephone or by calling into their offices. It doesn't matter who they are, so long as they're connected with property in some way. Tell them about yourself, what your ambitions are and what you're looking for. Exchange business cards. Follow up your chat with a phone call or email. Do the same on each of the next four days and you'll have a network of 25 people. Do the same next week, and you can get another 25. Soon you'll be at the centre of a web that's hundreds strong. Useful phone calls and emails will soon come winging their way in from the outermost reaches of your network.

> **Tomorrow, introduce yourself to at least five people that you don't know**

I've found that contacts I've made while networking have often turned into good friendships. Maybe that will happen to you, but don't let this distract you. You're not in this game to get loved. This is business. If you want a friend, get a dog. You're after success.

2 Auctions

Tell people you're looking for a good property deal, and lots of them will say they already know the best way to do this, ignore estate agents and head for an auction room. Here, supposedly, you'll find fantastic properties dumped by lazy, eager or otherwise over-motivated sellers that go for a song to the canny few. Well, up to a point. You can indeed hit the jackpot at an auction. It's true that going under the hammer will be properties sold off cheaply by lenders who want to dispose of repossessed homes and by people who just need to get cash fast. At auctions, however, you can also make catastrophic mistakes.

You should certainly go to auctions. They dispose of over 30,000 properties a year. They're fun, and you get a quick educational insight into what's going on in your area. As a spectator sport, they can't do you any harm. Watching the way the bidding goes will teach you a lot about market values. You can meet other property people to add to your network. And, if you go to enough auctions, you'll eventually alight upon a truly amazing deal.

Stick to the auction rules

However, you may be surprised to learn that many properties fetch not a penny less at auction than they would have done through an estate agent. You may be even more surprised to learn that many go for a good deal more. Part of the reason for this is that the strange atmosphere of a bidding war can push people into folly that they wouldn't otherwise be capable of. If you're going anywhere near an auction room, you've got to stick to the following rules:

 Do your homework. Although it's vital that you know precisely what you're going to bid for, it's surprising how many people go to auctions without carrying out basic research. Get the catalogue. Research the local market. Make sure your solicitor carries out local and national searches, checks title and tenure, and winkles out any restrictive covenants. You'll need a survey as with any other property, and you need to take account of any structural issues that emerge when deciding how much to bid.

Get on top of auction regulations. Usually there'll be a reserve price on any property, which will ensure that property remains unsold if this price isn't reached. So long as this price has been exceeded, you'll be the successful buyer if you're the highest bidder when the hammer falls. This will mean you're legally required to pay the price you've bid. You'll have to produce 10 per cent of the cost of the property before you leave the auction, and you'll have to pay the rest in full within 28 days.

Watch out for hidden costs. You'll have to pay for surveys, legal advice and stamp duty just as with any other purchase, but the auctioneer may also demand a 'buyer's premium' equivalent to 1.5 per cent of the purchase price. There's usually an administration fee, typically £150, payable to the auctioneer. Check the small print. Sometimes sellers demand that buyers pay for their auction fee and for their own legal work.

Make a reconnaissance trip. Before you go on a buying mission, visit a few times. Until you've absorbed the atmosphere of the auction room, you won't really know how to perform to best advantage. This game is trickier than it looks.

Look out for unsold lots. Where there have been no bidders, or the reserve price hasn't been reached, both the vendor and the auctioneer will be keen to sell, and may do an attractive deal with you afterwards.

Set a limit to what you're prepared to pay. This is the most important rule of all. Then you have to stick to it, however frenzied the bidding gets. Once the bidding goes above your limit, walk away. Always. You won't regret it.

Hold back. There's no need to bid until the auctioneer says 'Going once... going twice...' Letting everyone else show his or her hand will give you information; you don't need to return the favour. Watch out for auctioneers who take bids 'off the wall' – that is, make up fictitious bids until the reserve price is reached.

Don't compete. For you, an auction isn't a game in which you try to 'beat' rivals. If someone's fighting you hard, try raising your bids by small amounts to take the heat out of the situation. If that doesn't work, get out.

Be dispassionate. There's no room for covetousness, machismo, egotism, infatuation or recklessness in an auction room. Any of them could cost you plenty. Make sure you stay cool and calculating at all times.

Learn to be persistent. If you don't get the property you want, however much you may have set your heart on it, just come back another day. There are always more pebbles on the beach and more fish in the sea. Don't feel that because you've lost the property you want, you've got to buy another before you leave the auction room. These days there are plenty of auctions. Another one will be along soon.

3 Estate agents

Everyone hates estate agents. You, however, should make them your friends. Love them, relate to them, and make them feel special. All they're interested in is introducing willing sellers to willing buyers. Doesn't that make them your kind of people? Some of them aren't actually as unscrupulous as everyone thinks. They can be hard-working and honest. If they like to drive a hard bargain, that's just what you want to do as well. Remember, they have a tough life. There aren't many jobs as stressful as theirs. And if you can get some of them on your side, they may or may not help you find your life-changing deal, but they can be extremely useful when you yourself need to make a sale.

> **Once they've decided they like you, they'll bend over backwards to help**

Property information

Estate agents can be an invaluable source of information. Before you buy, whomever you're buying from, ask them what sells best in the area, and what improvements you might make that will add value. You can get all this information free from agents. Once they've decided they like you, they'll bend over backwards to help, and not just because they love you, of course – this is one of those reciprocal relationships that benefit both sides.

Agents are used to being despised, so they'll be that much more pleased if you treat them with a bit of the respect that they so often deserve. I send them bottles of champagne every Christmas. I take them out for lunch. I speak to them seriously. I don't hassle them. I pay their fees willingly when I think that they're going to give me the kind of service I want. I promise them that if they find me a property I'll sell it through them when the time comes. I don't use agents who provide a worse service for lower fees. The estate agent's charge is well worth paying if they are going to provide you with a good sale. In fact, I increase their fees.

All estate agents are motivated sellers. If they don't do deals, they won't make their own mortgage payments. You want to find the ones who are most motivated of all, the ones with a hunger to sell. Build up a relationship with them, and they'll open their hearts to you, and, more important, they'll open their property lists, which can be pure gold!

Negotiate with agents

Nonetheless, there's a downside to using agents. To attract sellers, they often promise them they'll get a better price than their rivals. To deliver on such pledges, they'll need to get more than the true market value. To secure the price you want, expect to do a lot of negotiating. You'll also find yourself competing fiercely for any decent property, since agents will be more firmly plugged into the market than any other kind of seller. If they're any good, they'll be peddling their wares in everything from glossy brochures to the local papers, and via the Internet they'll be reaching potential buyers far away from their own premises. Expect any really good properties coming on to an agent's books to be snapped up in seconds. And don't expect to get a really good bargain through an agent.

Like any other buyer, you have to look out for estate agents' tricks. When an agent calls you to say a property has just come onto the market, make sure he isn't just trying to fob you off with something that won't sell. Sometimes, stale properties are deliberately taken off the market briefly so they can be brought back on as hot stuff. If you watch an agent's list closely, you may spot properties you remember seeing before. Or, you may spot something new that you've seen before in another agent's window. The seller has changed agents because the property was sticking on the market.

When you've realised that a property isn't selling, but you think you can make it desirable, go in for the kill. For an agent, any sale is better than no sale. I always ask the agent who is the most desperate seller on their books. The agent is on a percentage, so she may do your work for you when it comes to beating down the seller of a sticky property.

> **Any sale is better than no sale**

④ Walkabout

You can, of course, cut out the estate agent simply by doing his or her work yourself. That way, a seller may give you a better price because she won't have to pay an estate agent's fee, and she won't have had her expectations inflated by an agent eager to get her business. So get on the road and see what you can find.

Keep searching

Ask yourself questions. Why is that place boarded up? What's that skip doing there? Why is that house empty? That bungalow has three estate agents' boards outside it. What might that mean? Perhaps that the owner is having difficulty shifting it. Most of the properties in one street have been extended, but not this one. Why might that be? Here's a small house on a large plot. Time to release its potential? All of these questions can uncover motivated buyers.

> **Get to know your chosen area in as much detail as you possibly can**

While you're looking, talk to people. Ask them questions, too. They might know what's available; they're bound to know a lot about the area. They may tell you squatters wrecked a certain house. Great. Remember, as I've said before, you're always looking for the worst house in the best street.

Make direct contact with the potential seller

Once you've found a property you're interested in, you've got to get hold of the owner. Knock on the door. If there's no answer, drop a note through the letterbox explaining your interest. If the property looks unoccupied, ask the neighbours who the owner is and where they can be found. Often they'll not only know the answer, but also be able to give you a complete history of the property. If that fails, send a letter to the house by post, it might be redirected. Finally, you can try the local council, who'll have a detailed registry showing the names of the owners of all properties. However, these may be inaccurate, and you'll still have to find contact details, so personal inquiries are definitely the best route.

When you've found the owner, try to make sure you deal with them directly. Direct contact is always more likely to produce a deal. Even when you're dealing with estate agents, it's often a good idea to get hold of their clients yourself and negotiate directly without the third party in the middle.

The key to walking or driving yourself to a deal is to make sure you don't miss opportunities. Get to know your chosen area in as much detail as you possibly can. Values can sometimes differ by 30 per cent from one street to another. Make sure you know which street is which.

Finally, keep your wits about you. Real bargains may lie in rough areas. In some of them, you might not want to get out of your car, and you might certainly worry about what would happen to it if you left it parked. You might want to take someone with you. Once when I was looking at a flat at the top of a tower block in Glasgow, I looked down to see a group of people round my car. I looked on in amazement as they broke into it and drove off. It was raining, it was one of the roughest parts of the city. You can imagine how pleased I was (not). Be careful out there.

5 Property finders

Many property professionals rely on networks of people who find suitable opportunities for them. Some of these are experienced specialists. They may well know their stuff better than you, and they'll have the opportunity to get on top of specialist fields. They charge a finder's fee, which is usually between 1 and 2 per cent of the purchase price. There are plenty of these people, although you may have to work quite hard to find them. They're elusive and skulking by nature, though they're usually honest enough. They rarely advertise their services. Estate agents often know who they are, and can help you find them.

I use several finders. The great advantage they offer is that they can free up your time, giving you space to analyse deals and work out which are really the best. If you can get the donkey–work done successfully for not much more than 1 per cent, you shouldn't complain. Also, they can expand your reach. The more properties, names, phone numbers and planning decisions they can bring you, the wider your range of choice will be.

However, you shouldn't pay for introductions unless you actually purchase the property, or you'll be incentivising your finder to bring you rubbish. Make sure your finders don't get into conflict with other finders. Once, two finders brought me the same property, and both wanted me to pay them.

Remember that it's going to be you making the eventual deal, not your finder. You can't ever rely on anyone else's judgement completely. Whenever a finder brings you something, however much you trust him or her, make sure you do your own homework, does it meet your five key criteria? Check out every detail yourself, whatever the finder tells you. Remember, they want the deal to go through to get their percentage. They are not going to have to live with the consequences.

6 Newspapers and magazines

There's no easier and cheaper way to find a bargain than to look through the 'properties for sale' section of a local newspaper. I've certainly uncovered many interesting deals in this way. Even if you don't find a life-changing deal, you can find much else that's useful. You can see at a glance what's available in what area and what the ranges of prices are. Put the paper in your pocket, get into your car and go looking.

The people who advertise in newspapers may have different motivation from those who use estate agents. They may have a strange piece of land or a building that isn't a standard residential property and which therefore offers particular opportunities for development. They may just want to sell quickly or quietly. Or, they may not want to pay an estate agent; some papers let you advertise your property for free.

As well as advertising individual properties, newspapers can provide signposts to other areas of inquiry. They may have advertisements for forthcoming auctions. They provide notices of planning permission applications and awards. They'll tell you about bankruptcies and deaths. Some people, 'the vultures' I call them, make a speciality of finding out when people die, and then hunting their houses down and making an offer, since their inheritors may want to make a quick sale. Sounds a bit morbid for you? Come on, these guys make fortunes! Life goes on and these guys make a profit.

Don't forget to read news stories, either. If a new transport interchange has been approved, now's the time to check out the area. Once it's up and running and boosting values skyward, you'll have missed the bus.

Of course, you can also do your own advertising. I've advertised for houses, buildings and land. I've had an overwhelming response. Simply put an advert in a local newspaper saying what kind of property you're looking for. Suggest you're prepared to pay top whack for exactly what you want. Use your networking team of property finders and make them your best friends.

The magazines you will need

There are certain periodicals that you should look at just to keep yourself abreast of the overall scene. The *Estates Gazette*, *Property Weekly* and *Which Property?* advertise property every week, including plots of land that would never make their way to an estate agent. They also offer all kinds of tips and advice that make them an essential reference tool. You'll find that these magazines grow more useful as you become a more advanced developer, but although such papers may at first seem to be targeting only the big boys, you'd be surprised how many small deals can still be found within their covers.

7 The Internet

Websites have, of course, begun to displace newspapers as a means of advertising property. But, in my view, we haven't seen anything yet. I'm sure the Internet will eventually change the way we buy and sell property completely. Already you can have a virtual 3D tour of both the inside and outside of any property before you ever go near it. That will make it possible to view a hundred properties a day without ever leaving your sofa. You'll be able to see them in real time. Soon you'll be able to interact with the property's owners, and ask them those crucial questions before you ever make a visit.

Become a research expert

Meanwhile, the Internet is already a wonderful research tool. All that effort that used to go into identifying areas, streets and market values can now often be replaced by the click of a mouse on a postcode.

There are bargains to be had on the Internet, though they're few and far between. The obvious reason for this is that you'll be competing with vast numbers of potential buyers all over the country, and perhaps the world. The very ease of use that the Internet offers undermines the advantage you might otherwise achieve by being more diligent than your rivals. In fact, I've never managed to buy anything from a website. You may find that the Internet proves to be a much better way of selling your property than of buying it. There are just too many lazy people using this method and snapping up anything that looks like a bargain.

The best way of finding a bargain is to go on those sites where people are advertising their own properties, rather than to use estate agents' sites. That way, you've got a chance of avoiding fees, and a better chance of speaking directly to the seller. Largely because of the Internet, 5 per cent of people are already direct sellers, and this figure is expected to rise to at least 25 per cent, as people grow more confident about property and understand it better.

8 Public records

The National Archive (which used to be called the Public Record Office) is one of the limited number of things that the Government provides that can actually help you. You've paid your taxes, use those records. They can tell you about site ownership, about the sales that have taken place, and what values have been achieved. Much of what they offer is free. Staff will be ready to help you, just tell them what you're looking for. If you play dumb, they may help you even more. Often you won't need to go into an office at all, you can simply use the Internet.

The Probate Service deals with 'non-contentious' probate business (where there is no dispute about the validity of a will or entitlement to take a grant); its records can alert you to probate properties, that have no owner, and are sold on the Crown's behalf by the council. The Crown is the ultimate owner of all land, and 'freeholders' just have a kind of tenure. So, when no freeholder can be found for any reason, a property reverts to the Crown. Usually, a council will just want to get rid of such properties as quickly as possible. They're usually run down and need substantial refurbishment, which means they are undervalued and just what you're looking for.

Public records also document repossessions by mortgage lenders. These offer another opportunity to buy at less than market value, since the borrower will still remain liable for the remainder of his debt, whatever price the property fetches. I know of a case in which a financial institution sold a repossessed house for 40 per cent less than market value. Look out for these particularly after interest rates have gone up when many people will be unable to keep up their mortgage repayments.

Of course, in this area, you'll need empathy and understanding to help the victims of personal tragedy. The fact that the squeamish may balk at this only gives you more of a chance. At the same time, the unique opportunities presented can sometimes inspire intense competition. Beware of getting carried away and paying more than a property would have been worth if picked up through an estate agent.

9 The planning system

Another publicly provided facility offering incredibly detailed information of great value to you is the planning system. Anyone seeking to extend or adapt any property, or change its use on any significant scale, has to ask permission from the local authority. The council has to make all of these applications and their outcomes available to the public. Often it will provide this information online.

Visit your local planning office

If you visit your local planning office, you can find out about all the pending applications for planning permission, and all those that have recently been granted or refused. Once again, helpful staff will probably be keen to assist you. With their help, you can analyse the applications that interest you most. Perhaps someone has applied to turn a house into four flats or to build a self-contained extension.

Once you've identified applications that appear to imply opportunities, you can contact whoever made the application. If in doubt, go to the architect whose contact details are listed on the application. Often they'll have submitted the application and the plans themselves.

When you've collected a set of possibilities, get to the owners and see if they want to sell. A high proportion of them will. Not everybody is putting up that extension to provide a bedroom for an unexpected baby. Lots of people are eager to squeeze as much value as possible out of their homes, and having secured planning permission for development they may be only too happy for somebody else to take over the work and risk involved in making it happen.

> **Keep a particular lookout for refused applications. The owner of the property may be disheartened after a long fight with the council**

It's a good idea to devise a letter explaining to people who've just secured planning permission exactly what you've got to offer them. Tell them you've seen their application (which you're quite entitled to do), and that it appears to create an opportunity that you're well placed to exploit. If you don't hear anything back, it's only cost you a stamp.

Once again, though, you mustn't get carried away. Even if you've got a start on the competition, you've still got to do the calculations that prove you've really found a life-changing deal. And don't be too taken by the content of the applications you find. You may be able to put in a better application yourself, once you've persuaded an owner to sell.

Keep a particular lookout for refused applications. The owner of the property involved may be disheartened after a long fight with the council, and therefore keen to sell. You, however, may be able to see how a different application might get past the council and make just as much money as his would have done.

Research planning legislation

As in the National Archive, you can pick up much useful general information in planning departments. The more you know about the incredibly complicated planning legislation that controls all development, the better you'll be able to judge your chances of making the enhancements that you may want to make yourself. Getting planning permission is an absolutely crucial skill for those seeking to make that million, and the more you know about the process the better.

10 New developments

New developments offer a rich source of below-market value purchases. Where a developer is trying to sell a lot of units at once, there are points at which his weakness will provide you with an opportunity. However, you have to strike at the right time.

> **You could make a considerable profit while your property is still being built**

Buying off-plan

The first moment to look out for is the one that will make you an early bird. In the early stages of a multiple development, lots of capital will be tied up, lots of loan interest will probably be being paid, and cash will be short. To alleviate this situation, the developer may be eager to get some cash quickly. You can help him, and yourself, by buying 'off-plan', at a discount.

Your cash will enable the developer to get going on his next project. Typically, you may pay 10 to 15 per cent less than you would when the properties are finished. If you're lucky, and the market is hot, you could make a considerable profit while your property is still being built. Plenty of people have done just that. As the first on the scene, you'll be able to pick off the best–quality units. If they're all built on the same plan, some will still have better views or more convenient access.

The second moment when developers are vulnerable to your interest is when they're at the very end of their sale process. Speak to developers directly; don't go through agents. They'll have flooded the market with identical properties and may well have saturated it. The worst properties may be sticking, yet it's from these properties that they'll have to make their profit. They just want to get out. These are the conditions in which you can make the last-minute pounce.

I once bought a property that was on offer for £1 million. I went to the developers with the cheeky offer of £650,000. They laughed at me, but I told them I had the money and could move quickly. Four weeks later they rang, and I got the house for £750,000. I could have sold it immediately for £850,000, and a few years later it was worth over a million – nice!

There are companies that specialise in finding off-plan or 'fag-end' properties for you. Sometimes, however, they over-inflate values, and you can end up with something that's not such a magic deal as you might think. As usual, you mustn't let the idea that you're getting a bargain put you off making your vital calculations.

11 Marketing yourself

Bill Gates was asked recently what he'd spend with his last dollar – assuming it was all the money he had left. His answer was 'marketing'. In any kind of business, you can't hope to get anywhere without promoting yourself better than the rest. If you look like a tomfool your career is over – presentation is everything. And this doesn't just apply when it comes to selling your property; it applies when you're buying as well. Turn up at an estate agent's looking like a tramp, and your offer may not even be passed on to the seller.

In any kind of business you can't hope to get anywhere without promoting yourself better than the rest. If you look second-rate, you will probably come second – and you won't have a career in property development. If you want to make money in this business, it helps to look smart. The impression you give is your calling card – it may seem superficial, but it makes a difference.

I used to turn up at estate agents and building sites in a clapped-out Vauxhall Astra, belching black smoke, but it didn't help me close any deals. Nowadays, I drive up to a site in either my top-of-the-range Porsche or my X5, because I want to create an impression. I know it sounds flashy, but I want people to know that I can buy a site that costs millions and they should take me seriously. I also make sure I'm wearing a nice suit and look healthy and well-groomed. It's all part of encouraging people to view me as someone worth doing business with, someone who is successful, because success breeds success. Look sharp, it works!

If you're going to be taken seriously, you also need good–quality stationery: decent business cards and headed paper, a proper name for your business, and a logo. When you make an offer, you've got to look credible. You may think you can't afford what's involved, and it's true that if you go to fancy designers they'll happily gobble up a lot of your money. In fact, the templates provided by the software that probably came with your computer are good enough to get you going.

" When you make an offer, you've got to look credible ""

We've seen that you can use newspapers to advertise your needs. Get your own website as well. The Internet is going to be everybody's shop window in the future. Putting up a site costs hardly anything nowadays, and I've certainly got a huge number of leads from my own (www.richlandgroup.co.uk). A website is vastly more important than a flashy brochure or a glamorous head-quarters building, yet it costs a great deal less.

Mapping systems

Your final route to finding that magic deal is a virtual one. Today, you can conduct your search from space, entirely free of charge. If you do so, you can come across opportunities that you'd find no other way.

You may already be familiar with Google Earth (www.googleearth.com). It's not, however, just something to amuse yourself with, it's a powerful property tool. Just download it (for free) and see. With its help, you can look at your chosen area and identify homes on big plots of land or with big back gardens, and pieces of land that you could put together to turn into a development site. You can see where access could be created, and where it couldn't. Nobody can stop you snooping on them.

All you have to do is spot your opportunity, switch to the street-map version, and you're on your way. There's a lot of money to be made in what those who don't like it call town-cramming. In Southfields, in South London, I once bought the back garden of a big manor house and built four houses on it.

 Google Earth isn't the only mapping system you can use. Promap (www.promap.co.uk) offers you immediate access to all of Bartholomew's and the Ordnance Survey's maps and aerial photography of the UK. It's much more detailed than Google Earth, and enables you to locate, view, measure, customise, print and export almost anything, although unlike Google there is a fee.

Whereas Google may give you an idea, Promap will show you precise boundaries. It will give you codes so you can look things up in the Land Registry and find out ownership, all online. Most of the property professionals think that it's well worth the money. And new mapping systems are still coming onto the market.

Those then are the dozen routes to finding your life-changing deal. Your task is to use as many of them as possible, as often as possible, and as regularly as possible. You'll then find out which of them have the most to offer in your particular situation. You've got to get out there and start looking *today*! Look at the twelve-week property plan starting on page 179. I expect over the coming weeks that you will have viewed no less than 30 properties within your price range, in a great location, with a clear target market, with scope to add value and that fits your time-scales. From that list you will find several that will make you money.

OK, let's assume you've found what you consider to be the deal of the century, the next question is – does it really stack up? The following chapter explains what boxes you need to tick to find out. Following this advice is critical to whether you become a success or not!

Do the figures stack up?

...take off the rose-tinted glasses, it's got to make financial sense!

Making the figures stack up is something that I have learnt the hard way. When I started in property development I had a disaster that nearly put me out of business. I bought a development and I didn't double-check the figures. I relied on a third party telling me what the finished properties would sell for, and accepted at face value a list from an estate agent supporting the price. Unfortunately, when it came to selling the properties, it became clear to me that the figures were wrong – the estate agent had inflated the price by more than 20 per cent. Which meant I developed a two-year property project for no profit. And the reason I screwed up so badly was because I didn't check that the figures stacked up properly!

Later on I discovered that the person who was selling me the site was also a silent partner of the estate agency that gave me the misleading valuations in the first place. I took my eye off the ball and I paid the consequences.

Now, I don't want you to do the same, and that's why this next section is absolutely critical to whether you become a success or not. Assess whether your deal can make money with these three essential elements:

1 Work out your profit

2 Take off your rose-tinted glasses

3 Get the budget right

So now you've spent several weeks identifying what you hope is the deal of a lifetime, the one that will launch you into the premier property league; you're about to become a player. As I've said earlier, at this point the key thing you must ask yourself is 'Will your deal make money?'

This is the crux of all your hard work. We all know that money isn't everything, but ultimately your business has to make a profit for you to be successful. You can't even think of running a business without making a profit. Later in the book I will show you how to create a detailed residual valuation where you plan the cash flow of your business to the penny. But now you need to do a 'back of the envelope' calculation to make sure the deal stacks up. You will need to work out the total revenue you can get from your scheme, less the cost of your site, stamp duty, fees, and construction and refurbishment costs. Within this basic calculation you will take off bank interest and that will give you a profit figure before tax.

You, too, can work out really quickly whether it's going to make money or not – and that's the very first thing you need to do. But, of course, there's something else you need to bear in mind – a lot of deals aren't done separately; they're done in conjunction with each other. So, you may find what looks like a great deal, but you need to still be looking for other deals. You need to be doing some very basic calculations: Does it make sense? Does it add up? Do this before you start spending money on surveyors, solicitors, lenders and builders. Let's start with the basics.

1 Work out your profit

You want to find out as quickly as possible if your deal makes money. Does it warrant spending loads of time, energy and resources on it? Start by appraising a potential property scheme financially. To work out if you are going to make a profit you need to know:

● The cost of the land/site/property?

● The total cost of the works (including contingency)?

● The cost of legal, borrowing and agent's fees?

● What you can sell the finished property for?

Add up your total costs and take this figure away from your selling price to give you the profit or Return on Capital Employed (ROCE).

For example, let's say you:

● Buy a site for £100k

● Your total costs are £100k

● You can sell for £250k

That means your profit is £50k, which equates to a return on capital of 25 per cent.

Right away this deal stacks up, and so I will now spend time looking at the figures in more detail. This tells you roughly what profit you can expect to make, and importantly, how much a site is worth. You should always aim for a return of 20+ per cent or more, and if it's less than that, you know you are paying too much for the site. It sounds simple but believe me, a lot goes into these figures, and as you will see later, get one wrong and you are in trouble! Master this skill and you can quickly work out how the deal – even huge deals – are going to perform.

2 Take off your rose-tinted glasses

In property deals, it's crucial that you do not let your emotions
rule you. Once you start thinking 'I've just fallen in love with this',
you're finished. Forget about love. You're looking at this in the
cold light of day. Does this deal make sense?

Sod's law: anything that can go wrong, will

The thing you should always remember with property developing
is that there are so many variables and something is bound to
go wrong – a plumber won't turn up; your builder's just stopped
coming to site, an unforeseen cost has appeared from nowhere.
But that won't faze you because you are already forewarned with
this knowledge. You have not just done your basic sums but
you've done your contingency planning – which we'll look at more
closely in the next few chapters. And, equally important, if and
when something goes wrong, *you* don't panic, you keep a cool
head because you know what you're doing.

You will already know that if you've got builders in – foreign
builders, UK builders, you name it – they never finish on time.
Most people who start out on property deals go into them with
their eyes shut. But not you. You will go in there with your eyes
wide open. So let's go through these figures in a bit more detail.

Calculate your projected revenue

The first jigsaw piece is Revenue. Working out your revenue is
easy. If you're doing a small-scale deal on a flat or a house, you
can get three estate agents in to tell you what the refurbished
property could sell for. We call it GDV – Gross Development Value,
which in lay terms means how much you can sell your total
development for. For example, if you have got ten flats that you
are going to sell for £100,000 each, your GDV is a million
pounds.

You can also work it out per square foot. In London, for example,
let's say the average price per apartment is £500 per square foot
(though that may vary widely across the UK). Work out the total
sellable square footage and multiply that by the price per square
foot. As a rule of thumb:

- 400–600 square feet is a one-bed apartment

- 600–900 square feet is a two-bed apartment

- Over 1,000 square feet is a three-bed apartment or penthouse

- A large house could be anything from 2,000 square feet plus

When working out the revenue, I would advise anyone not to include market inflation. Just make sure that it's right for now. You've got to be prudent and assume the market will drop rather than rise. Check the price now and hope that prices remain stable.

Calculate your basic costs

Having worked out your revenue you then need to estimate your costs. This includes building and post-completion costs, agent's fees, finder's fees (if using one), interest and legal fees. If you are selling you are responsible for providing a Home Information Pack (better known as 'HIPS'). The pack will include evidence of title, copies of planning agreements, local searches, guarantees for any work on the property, and an energy performance certificate. It will cost you between £400-800.

There is also the cost of the site and obviously that will involve negotiation into how much you want to pay for it, which is dealt with later in the book. But you can put down your ballpark figure, and you roughly know what you can sell the property for.

Stamp Duty

Don't forget to add the cost of Stamp Duty. Currently there is no Stamp Duty for any property valued up to £175,000 and, importantly, if at the moment you do a carbon neutral scheme now, you won't have to pay any Stamp Duty at all. This figure may increase if we have a change of political leadership.

- Stamp Duty on £175,001-250,001 is 1 per cent

- Stamp Duty on £250,000-500,000 is 3 per cent

- Stamp Duty on £500,001 and above is 4 per cent

Believe me, this is important! On a property valued at over a million pounds, you are going to be paying £40,000 in Stamp Duty.

Other fees

If you get planning permission for a development, the council may attach a document called a Section 106. This stipulates rules and conditions to provide affordable housing or to contribute monies to the local authority. In my eyes, a Section 106 is basically a tax on property developers. My advice is, if you buy sites with planning permission always ask whether there has been a Section 106 agreement and what it entails. Sometimes you may have to contribute towards building a new road, improving health and school facilities, creating an area for kids to play in, or contribute to listed gardens. Of course, providing affordable or social housing is important, as the government doesn't build council housing anymore; they expect us to do it!

Include your travel costs

How far should you travel for the right deal? Of course, it's a question of balance. Deals that involve travelling a long distance may still be worth doing, but if you're starting up they can be a lot of hassle. You've got to build in your travel costs, where you're going to stay, how you're going to find the labour, and how you find people in the locality when something goes wrong with your project. Your best deals may be next door.

3 Get the budget right

The biggest and most common mistake is getting your budget wrong. Most people do simple things like forgetting about the cost of Stamp Duty, or miscalculating the building costs. Believe it or not, they even forget they have to pay interest on money they borrow, or forget about bank fees or mortgage fees. In the end they'll lose money because, inevitably, property development is always going to cost more than they expect and it always takes more time than planned.

People seriously underestimate what the budget for a refurbishment will be. They underestimate or forget completely about agent's fees and legal fees when they sell.

Planning costs

How long is a piece of string? Planning costs can go through the roof if you are not careful. Architects' fees, consultants' fees and planning fees are all part of your planning costs. Now, if you're going to buy a property that you hope to change, the planning fee alone costs approximately £150+ per unit just to submit the application. This can vary and will depend on what you want to do.

You may need to take on a planning consultant and they can charge about £250 an hour, but they are usually worth every penny. They'll come in and give you quick advice on what you can and can't do. You can find your planning consultant through recommendations from your architect or quantity surveyor. Or you can find one on the Internet or in the *Yellow Pages*. You should always negotiate with them, but usually they charge by the hour. They have vast knowledge and know exactly within seconds what will and won't be permitted, what will be easy or difficult. They'll put you in the right steer from day one. If you're doing a complex scheme, you can use them to help you and your architect with your planning applications.

You may also need a tree consultant. These are people who are experts on trees and Tree Protection Orders. If you're going to buy a big site and you're going to put a planning application in, if the trees don't have a TPO on them, the council will send someone down within seconds to stamp TPOs and if you've got a tree (or anything with a leaf attached!) with a TPO you usually can't move it. Or, if you do, it costs a fortune and you'll have to replant it.

> **My view is that obtaining planning permission is potentially a licence to print money, but it can be a high-risk strategy**

My view is that obtaining planning permission is potentially a licence to print money, but it can be a high-risk strategy. It is a complex maze not only because it can be an expensive strategy if you get it wrong, but also because if the planners turn you down it is very frustrating and can set you back for several months.

By now you should have worked out, on paper, if your deal stacks up. Of the hundreds of potential deals that come across my desk, I find that over 90 per cent of them will not be profitable. Only if they stack up do I take the project to the next step, which is looking at the costs in detail – also known as a Residual Valuation. Remember, God is in the Detail. It is all about getting the detail absolutely right. Get it right and you can do very well. Get it wrong and don't bother giving up your day job. So read on, and let me show you how to cover every angle.

God is in the detail

...you must understand every single element of the deal!

I was once sitting with my architect going through all the pros and cons of a new property scheme. We've all heard the old saying 'the devil's in the detail', but he turned round and said, 'God is in the detail.' When architects consider their work, they know that their peace of mind comes with getting the detail right. I have shown you the elements you need to assess to see if your deal stacks up. Now you need to micro-analyse the deal, making sure that you have got all the costs right, before you start spending money.

Here are the essentials to consider:

1. Is it a refurbishment or a makeover?
2. Calculate your construction costs
3. The cost of borrowing: bank fees

Getting costs right is the number one thing people fall down on. You've got to understand the various costs that go into a new build or a refurbishment – your demolition costs, external costs, plumbing, electrics, heating, flooring, bathrooms, kitchens, insulation, soundproofing... you need to factor all these in to work out if you can make money from your potential deal. It really does help to employ a professional to look over your figures.

1 Is it a refurbishment or a makeover?

For me, a refurbishment (what we call a 'refurb' in the trade) means totally stripping out a whole property, getting right back to the bare bones and starting again. A makeover is different. You can do makeovers for a lot less – new flooring, a nice kitchen, and a new bathroom all cost less, and the costs are relatively easy to calculate.

In a rising market you can make good money doing makeovers, but if you want to be a property mogul you usually have to get into the big refurbishing projects and new builds to really add value. This involves putting in new electrics, plumbing, insulation and plastering. The list is endless depending on the scale of your project. It is not just stripping off old paper and adding a fresh coat of paint.

Recently, in a TV show with two would-be property developers who were refurbishing a house that was just over a thousand square foot, they said to me, 'Oh, we're going to do this for fifty grand.' I knew right away it was going to cost them about £150,000. They were shocked and didn't believe me. I was proved right in the end virtually to the last penny, and they lost a fortune.

> **If you want to be a millionaire you usually have to get into the big refurbishing projects and new builds**

You may be wondering whether these guys were optimistic or naïve. After all, £50,000 is a serious amount of money to spend refurbishing a house, but they made a mistake of costing a makeover; they had not realised that there was a structural problem in the house, as they didn't get a survey. They needed new electrics, plumbing, windows and heating; the list was endless. So they totally underestimated the costs in every way.

2 Calculate your construction costs

Construction costs for a new build project may be anywhere between £75 and £200+ a square foot. When refurbishing a property you can expect to pay anything from £75 to £150 a square foot. These are ball-park figures but act as good guidance.

Let's suppose you've bought a nice little property for £100,000 and hope to sell it for £200,000. £50,000 is your cost for development. You would therefore think, 'Oh well, that will make me £50,000 profit.' But with all the costs I've mentioned in the last chapter, your total costs may add up to more than you think!

As a very basic rule of thumb, if you want to apply just one figure that should cover you for everything that should include agent's fees, lawyer's fees and construction costs, I generally use a rough estimate of around £200 a square foot for new building work. I know it sounds like a lot, but it should cover you for everything. Refurbishment costs are not easily determined, as you may find yourself with hidden costs. Once you start digging out the joists, as I've done on a couple of projects, you may find your costs escalate. Whilst with a new build project you can know almost to the penny what your development is going to cost. A quantity surveyor can be employed to quantify the costs accurately.

> **With a new build you can know almost to the penny what your development is going to cost**

If you're putting in really high specification fittings and finishes, costs can go through the roof. However, every property is different. You have to make sure you factor in all the different scenarios in your costs. The point is, it is better to over-estimate and make sure you have enough to cover your project comfortably than what a lot of developers do – underestimate the figures and flatter the profit. One thing is for sure, it all comes out in the wash, and if you have missed any costs you can kiss goodbye to your profit.

Refurb hell

On one occasion I took on the refurb of a nursing home in Teddington. It looked great. A local builder I was purchasing from gave me advice, 'Oh yeah, the roof's fine, you'll be able to keep the roof.' I took his word for it, and on the surface it looked fine. At that point, of course, we should have got an expert surveyor to give me a professional opinion. Then we started working on it and discovered that the joists holding up the building were rotten, they all had woodworm and dry rot, and we had to replace them. Replacing them became an absolute nightmare because we had to support all the walls with support columns, which took loads of money, labour and time. We had to take out the joists one at a time and pay a specialist company to put them all back in.

Then we got to the roof, which, of course, was infested with woodworm. So we had to take the roof off, but the planners wanted us to keep the same tiles because they were old tiles – it was a listed building. This is what happens in refurbs, inevitably they're old buildings and they may be listed. So we had to keep all the old tiles and make them good, and then put the roof back. The whole cost was much more expensive than building new.

Another time, in Clapham, I went to build new and we did a full environmental survey. We'd dug several bore holes all around the site, but they'd somehow managed to miss asbestos that had been buried underground. It cost £250,000 to remove and put the project back by over three months. It all cost time and money and there weren't too many smiling faces for a while.

You have to be super-vigilant as crazy things can happen. In another project I did in Kingston, we found that the ground had subsidence that hadn't been picked up on the survey – it had virtually been impossible to detect it. We had to pour huge amounts of concrete in and build reinforced walls and retaining walls. It cost £200,000 on top of the budget, painful!

3 The cost of borrowing: bank fees

You must take into account bank arrangement fees, interest charges, and non-utilisation fees. Get your bank to explain these costs in detail because it is when you miss these details that your profits can be eaten away.

If you're a first-timer, the bank will want you to put personal guarantees on the line, which means that if the project goes pear-shaped, your life as you know it is over. Don't think the bank will be lenient with you; they will take the shirt off your back to pay their debt and may even make you bankrupt. Banks always want you to have what I call 'hurt money' in the project. In other words, you will suffer if you do not pay them back. You can negotiate with them, but they are not in the business of taking risks. Bank fees can add up very quickly and the longer the project takes the more money they can get.

So let's have a look at all the costs and calculations that could be on your list. Photocopy the next page and write your own figures alongside. Add up all your projected costs and subtract this figure from what you can sell it for. This is your profit.

Firstly, work out your Gross Development Value (GDV) i.e. the price at which you can sell your completed development for. This will then give you your total revenue which you should subtract the costs listed in the chart opposite from.

If your projected profit is over 20 per cent of your costs – great. It is time to move on to the next stage of your property development. However, if your projected profit is less than 20 per cent (unless you can add huge value somewhere else), forget about this deal and continue your search.

TOTAL REVENUE =

LESS:	
Cost of property or site	
Stamp Duty (see page 98)	
Purchase legal and survey costs	
Introduction agent's/finders' fees	
Section 106 costs	
Planning costs	
Bank arrangement fees	
Bank legal fees and interest costs	
Monitoring surveyor	
Construction costs (sq ft x cost/sq ft)	
Architect fees	
Engineer fees	
Project manager	
Quantity surveyor	
Marketing and advertising costs	
Buildings insurance	
Contingency fees	
Home Information Pack (HIP)	
Personal cash flow (money to live on)	
= PROFIT	£

Note: All fees are negotiable, but refer to chapter 13, 'Build your wealth team' on page 156 for typical costs.

All the work you have done so far is more or less in your own time, and your own time is free. As we move on to the next phase you are likely to incur costs from other professionals. You've got to double-check, you've got to triple-check, and you've got to make sure, above all else, that you haven't missed something out, because even one small thing that seems insignificant now can be the death nail in any deal. If you are satisfied with everything so far, now is the time to start spending money on the professionals.

More homework

...the big print giveth and the small print taketh away!

Just when you thought you'd done all your homework, it's time to take the next step. We call this stage 'detailed due diligence', which means you find out exactly what you're buying. This is important, because now you're going to have to pay for third parties like surveyors, solicitors and consultants. So before you get here, you want to be very sure that all the work that you've done in your own time tells you if it's worth spending more time, money and resources on this project. Now we are into spending cash.

Two women I worked with for a TV series bought a flat with a garden where they believed that the garden belonged to them. They thought the seller had implied this and the estate agency particulars did. They spent a fortune doing the garden up. When they tried to sell the property, the person buying it did proper legal due diligence and informed them that they did not own the garden. They were gobsmacked. It was true – the garden was a communal garden for all the flats, but they'd assumed it was theirs and had spent thousands doing it up. Their sale fell through. If you look carefully at estate agents' details you will see that they have got huge disclaimers making clear what they write is what the vendor told them and is not necessarily accurate. Check what you are contracted to buy and make sure your solicitor also checks it carefully as well.

Don't be tempted to cut corners, because it's a false economy. If you can't sell you can't make a profit and you can forget about your career as a property developer, never mind making money.

So, do your due diligence homework to ensure that what you are buying is what you think you are buying. Due diligence has several essential elements:

1. Buyer beware! Buy with your head, not with your heart
2. If it seems too good to be true, it usually is
3. Who really owns your property?
4. Surveys and searches
5. Use a quantity surveyor
6. Sometimes it's better to walk away

1 Buyer beware!

You have to make sure that what you are actually buying is what you think you are buying, and that there are no hidden problems with it. Check what the seller is telling you is true, that no one else has claim to the land, which means you have 'good title', that legally it stacks up, and, most important, that it stacks up financially.

There's a famous story about the American leisure group who

bought the former London Bridge some years back. The Americans thought they were buying the historic Tower Bridge and wanted it as part of a hotel theme park. They never checked what actual bridge they were buying. Anyway, somewhere in the Arizona desert stands a very boring old London bridge!

A lot of people buy properties wearing rose-tinted glasses. They get emotionally carried away with the idea of the property. It is so deeply ingrained in our subconscious minds that we've got to have shelter and territory and people get emotionally carried away with this. Often, the heart is driving the purchase rather than the brain. I've read that some women spend more time choosing a pair of shoes than they do choosing their flat or apartment. Needless to say, successful property investors buy with their head, not with their heart.

2 If it seems too good to be true, it usually is

I've looked at so many deals that seem absolutely amazing on first sight, sometimes even after going through the details. But for loads of reasons, the deal turns out not to be so good.

Say a property looks amazingly cheap for what it is – you need to ask yourself, what can you sell it for? It's easy to do this basic analysis quite quickly; you can call up estate agents, you can find out what properties have sold for in the area on the Internet, and work out what price you could sell for. You can also quickly assess what you should be paying for it, because you'll know the price of other similar properties. And if the asking price is a lot lower than it should be, ask yourself where the catch is? When you investigate you will find the main problem areas are usually with searches and legal covenants, or rights of way.

Make way for the bins

I had a friend who bought a house recently that was cheaper than the rest of the houses in the street. After he moved in he discovered that his neighbours had a right of way across his garden to wheel all their rubbish bins. His house was an end-of-terrace and there was a legal right of way right across his garden. About eight or nine houses used this one right of way, so it was a nightmare. The neighbours had the right just to tramp through his garden any time they wanted, which for security reasons devalued the house. The people who were selling kept it very quiet and made sure that he only viewed the property on days when the bins weren't there.

3 Who really owns your property?

The first question you want to ask is, is your property freehold or leasehold? Freehold means that you legally own and are responsible for the whole fabric of the property; it's entirely yours. It will be subject to any covenants or other laws in place such as planning law or conservation areas, but in the main you are free to do what you like with it.

Then there's leasehold. Leasehold means you've bought a lease that allows you to live in the property for a certain length of time. You don't own the property; you only own the right to live there. The actual owner is the person who owns the freehold. Leases can be relatively short or as long as 999 years, but no matter what the term is, the leasehold eventually reverts back to the freeholder when the term expires, unless you pay more to extend it. Recent legislation provides for the right to extend your lease, but you will have to negotiate a price for it with the freeholder.

Short leases can be good value, but if a lease is under 70 years, many mortgage companies don't like lending on them. A short lease is a depreciating asset, so a long leasehold is preferable.

The freeholder makes the rules

When you buy a leasehold you have to abide by the terms of the lease. The lease lists the things you must do regarding the upkeep of the property. Generally, you have a legal obligation to pay ground rent to the freeholder, and a set share of the service charges towards the maintenance of the building. You may also find that you can't put down the wooden floors you dreamt of, hang washing out, keep a pet, nor leave your bikes in the hallway. You can't sub-let without permission. If you are interested in buying a leasehold property, get your estate agent to supply you with a copy of the lease so you know what you will be committing to.

> **Get your estate agent to supply you with a copy of the lease so you know what you will be committing to**

With apartment blocks, both freehold and leasehold can cause problems. If you have bought a flat in a block that's split up into twelve apartments each with a share of the freehold, anything to do with the upkeep or improvement of common areas will have to be agreed by everybody. If people don't get on or have different objectives, it can be chaos. If it's a leasehold property you can take annoying neighbours to court if they're not abiding by the lease; when there's a freehold, there may be no actual agreement in place. Recent legislation has created a third type of ownership for flats called 'commonhold', but the legal precedents are still being worked out on this.

Most people prefer freeholds to leaseholds. If you have a leasehold, make sure that there is clear freeholders' documentation in place so that rules can be enforced.

It's hard to escape problems that stem from common ownership and proximity, so try to do as much 'soft' due diligence as you can by chatting up the porter if there is one, meeting prospective neighbours, and visiting the property at different times of day and evening. And always think about what will happen when you come to sell on.

Use your solicitor

The legal business of buying or selling a property is called 'conveyancing'. A good solicitor is worth his or her weight in gold. Ask your solicitor to check everything. Every property leaves fingerprints behind and over the years it's documented very carefully. A solicitor will spot if there are any issues that you need to be aware of. If you don't already have a solicitor, my advice is to get recommendations from friends.

Some firms use legal clerks to do the routine work, so make sure you know who is representing you. If your deal has anything unusual in it, it pays to have expertise.

Your solicitor's first act will be a Land Registry search to determine that the seller has the right to sell the property. Recently, a major financial institution in London was conned out of a £1m deposit on the supposed sale of a famous central London hotel. It was worth between £400m and £600m. The institution put down a non-refundable £1m deposit in a conman's account believing that the owners had given him the right to sell their hotel. Even the biggest financial institutions in the world can be conned by smooth-talking if they do not do their due diligence.

> ❝ A search might reveal limitations on what you can do with the property ❞

Restrictions and covenants

The solicitor also carries out various other searches to ensure that no alterations have been made without planning permission. If you buy something that is in breach of a legal planning requirement, for instance – if someone has built a huge extension without planning permission – the council can come and ask you to knock it down. The search will also check if there any restrictive covenants or rights of way, ensuring all the boundaries are clear, and that there are no outstanding options on the land.

It's very important to do these searches thoroughly because when you buy something, you're taking over any pre-existing liability. A search might reveal limitations on what you can do with the property. I know properties with restrictive covenants in place where you cannot get planning permission on the land to build more than one house. If you've bought a house with a massive back garden, thinking that you can develop the garden, and then you find out there's a restrictive covenant over it, you will not be best pleased.

'Right to light' is a legal right – you can't build a development or extension and block someone's light. Check that your development will not block anyone's light.

You can insure against some ancient restrictive covenants where the ownership of the covenant is often lost in time and the risk of someone coming along and claiming against you is remote.

4 Surveys and searches

There are different types of surveys depending upon your situation and the age and condition of the property you plan to purchase. You can choose from:

Basic Valuation. Banks and mortgage companies will require a valuation survey. This is an inspection on behalf of the mortgage lenders to ensure the investment is sound. A valuation is not a structural survey; it provides no legal recourse and is for the benefit only of the lender. All it does is let the lender know that what they're giving the money for is worth at least the amount they are lending you.

Homebuyer's Survey and Valuation Report (HSV). This is a basic survey carried out in a standard format by the Royal Institution of Chartered Surveyors (RICS). The surveyor will look at issues like damp, dry rot, the state of the roof and the walls, and provide a report on the status of your property. It also gives you full legal recourse to claim against problems not spotted by the surveyor.

Full Structural. Recommended for listed buildings, properties built before 1900, any building constructed in an unusual way, a property you are planning to renovate, and properties that already have extensive alterations. It gives you legal recourse.

Environmental. If you purchase a site with environmental contamination, even if it's leakage from elsewhere or an underground stream that brings debris to your site, you as the new owner will be responsible for getting the site cleaned and tested. This can be very time-consuming and costly!

Specialist. Some planning permissions have conditions requesting an archaeological, ecological, or contamination survey. You will have to pay for a specialist survey or to assess whether your development will create problems for local wildlife or environmental concerns. Sometimes you find out about these the hard way.

There was the time when I didn't carry out an ecological survey. It would have checked if there was any rare wildlife on the site. It was scrub land and naïvely I assumed that it was fine. It turned out that a rare bat and twelve types of rare insect lived on the land, and I ended up having to commission an ecological report that cost £25,000. The ecologist set traps and tested all the insects and it took three months to get the tests back. Planning permission was delayed, and the site that had looked so attractive was suddenly an absolute nightmare.

A friend of mine owned a huge site where he had to stop development because of a nesting pair of sandmartins. I was also involved in an office development where they found an endangered toad on the site. The whole scheme had to be stopped as tunnels were built for the toads to go across the road.

Once we bought an old warehouse in the City of London. The builders began work and started digging, and then they started finding bones – human bones. We called the police, and the police called in the archaeologists, who announced that we had bought a two thousand-year-old Roman graveyard. And all works had to be stopped on this site for over a year. The entire site was documented. In the end, we had to lay a layer of disinfected, bacteria-free silicon white sand over the whole site, and build a raft foundation over it before we could build our building on top. It cost an extra £4m – oops! So check before you buy.

5 Use a quantity surveyor

Difficult to check for these things

To understand your costs properly, you should employ a quantity surveyor who is there to analyse in detail, line by line, every single item your property development will require. Remember that refurbs are difficult because so often you're dealing in the realms of the unknown. You can get covered for hidden issues, but those types of surveys are very expensive.

It's a false economy not to use a quantity surveyor – even if only to look over your proposed financial plan and say, 'You're a bit light there, you're a bit heavy there.' The Royal Institution of Chartered Surveyors' book *The Property Makeover Guide*, updated annually gives advice on the cost of anything that you'd expect to have to pay, whether for a plumber, a builder, repointing, etc.

If you are borrowing money from the bank, they will probably want their own surveyor – known as a monitoring surveyor – to

note what you're doing and what your surveyors are doing.
A monitoring surveyor reports back to the bank, basically acting like a hawk over what you're doing. They check that you're doing it right, asking lots of questions. If there's anything wrong they report it to the bank or discuss it with the architect or your various project managers. You can be sure that if there's anything untoward going on, the monitoring surveyor will let the bank know immediately. The cost of a monitoring surveyor varies and can be agreed with the banks depending on the size of the job.

6 Sometimes it's better to walk away

And finally, sometimes you may have to walk away from a deal, even though it looks like the deal of the century. If you do your proper due diligence and it throws up huge issues, don't be afraid to walk away because there's always another deal. Never be in a rush to buy. You know this from Chapter 6 – the whole point of doing your homework is to discover if you can make a profit. If you want to be a millionaire, don't rush in if the costs and detailed due diligence don't stack up!

In property development many activities take place simultaneously. While you are working on your homework you may find yourself negotiating to buy the property. Once you've carried out your full due diligence there will always be issues that can change the value of the deal. Perhaps, like my TV friends, you might have found out that you don't own the garden, or that there is a right of way across your property. How does that affect the value of your life-changing deal? Do you walk away or negotiate an even better deal? That's what I am going to explain in the next chapter. What you learn quickly in property development is that every stumbling block is a potential stepping-stone to a better deal.

Negotiate and close the deal

...make sure you get the very best deal possible every time!

Information is power. Your due diligence will give you the information you need to negotiate the best deal possible – you can use any problems you have discovered and highlight them to reduce the price you pay.

Negotiation is a skill that makes a lot of people feel uncomfortable because you have to play hardball. Try and think of it as a game - business is like sport. When you're on the field in sport, you're going to play to win, as long as you play within the rules. When I'm at the negotiating table, it is as if I'm on the field playing ball; I want to score as many goals as I can.

If you feel uncomfortable about negotiating, then I am sorry but the property business is not for you. But I think if you've read this far in the book, you're still in the game. You must push for the best possible deal because your profit is what's going to set up your business and change your life.

This chapter is about the art of negotiating your deal and bringing it to a close. There are four key steps: research; negotiation; making sure the deal is watertight; and closing the deal. Negotiating a deal is an art in itself, but here are the essentials:

1. Be a detective: find out all you can about your seller or buyer
2. Know your leverage: choose your throw-aways
3. Understand their price
4. Start low
5. Keep it positive: they may come back
6. Make the deal bigger
7. Closing the deal
8. Get your legal arrangements in order
9. Completion
10. What not to do

1 Be a detective

The key to successful negotiation is to find out all you can about the other side's motivation. Be willing to walk away from the deal if it looks like going wrong. There's always another deal. Deals are like buses; another one will be along in fifteen minutes.

Be a detective. Understand the other side's needs and wants. The more information you have about someone, the more you know what motivates him or her to sell. The more you understand that motivation, the better chance you have of getting the deal you want. Find out as much about their aims as you can. I try not to interrogate. It's like building up a jigsaw. What do the sellers really want? What are their reasons for selling? Why have they brought it to the market? Why are they not developers themselves? It may not just be about price. Make sure you know everything about the area. It could be that the sellers need to move quickly and they're desperate for the money, they're fed up with the site, or they are moving for school catchment.

Start with the agents, but bear in mind that what agents often tell you is not the right answer. Agents have other motivations – their fee, or maybe another buyer in the background.

Don't talk to the monkey, talk to the organ grinder

Meet the seller as soon as possible and establish a rapport. Who is he or she? Why is he selling? What else is he doing in his life? How much money is he worth? When people feel they're dealing with somebody they can trust, who is not going to mess them around, you've a better chance of closing the deal. I always try to meet the seller before I start negotiating, to test the water and look into the whites of his or her eyes.

Trust your instincts

Sometimes you have to trust your instincts and walk away. The deal might all stack up, but you just smell a rat. You don't know what it is but your subconscious is telling you that something is not right. Whenever that happens to me, I listen to my instinct, which is usually correct.

2 Know your leverage

Think about what you're bringing to the table. It's not always just about money. What is it that this person wants that you can give him? Does he want to move fast, does he want a joint venture, and does he want some money now, some later? Does he want to keep his credibility in the deal, or does he want a silent partner? And he also wants to know, can you do it? Remember my point about personal presentation (see page 90). They need to see somebody credible; someone who they believe can do the deal.

Once I was negotiating with a guy who was also doing another different deal, which would make him even more money. He needed cash quickly for his bigger deal, so he wasn't too worried about our smaller negotiation. He just wanted a speedy conclusion to secure the bigger deal. At times like that you can make a low offer and it will be accepted. In fact, I am shocked at how many times I have put in a very low offer and it has been accepted.

There are always people who will agree the most ridiculous price because they're desperate. For example, a family have been left a property and all they want to do is dispose of it as quickly as possible – if you can say 'I've got the money and I can pay in a week' it might be a couple of hundred grand less than they think the property is worth, but for them a bird in the hand is worth two in the bush. They may do the deal with you.

Choose your throw-aways

There are always some areas to discuss that you don't care about. Write them down and put them on the table to lose. For example, you know you're going after a property with dry rot, but you're going to replace the wood anyway in your refurbishment; use the dry rot as one of the chips to give away. The seller and agent don't know that it doesn't affect your valuation.

3 Understand their price

As part of your research, ask yourself: Why do they want this amount? Why do they think it's worth this price? And, crucially: what will it take for them to do the deal? There's always a figure someone will accept, and a figure they won't accept, so somewhere in the middle is where you're going to agree a deal. Try and get it just above the price they won't accept.

Read the body language

Notice the body language of the person you are talking to. If the body language is open, they are open for a deal. Or are they closed against you? What are their advisers doing? How are they looking at each other?

4 Start low

Start your negotiation really low. I always go in really low because I want to see what their reactions are. If people aren't screaming down the phone to me, 'Who the hell do you think you are putting in a price like that?' I always feel I've put in too high a price. There is nothing worse than when I put in a really low price and the vendor comes back with an acceptance. I should have tried at a lower price, or perhaps there is something seriously wrong with the property? Of course, if you think you can add a lot of value to the property, you just have to go straight in at the asking price. Every deal is unique but I usually start negotiating at least 20 per cent below the asking price, although if I think I can add serious value I may sometimes go in at the full price to take the property off the market, it really depends on all the circumstances.

5 Keep it positive

Don't be afraid to walk away from a negotiation. Rarely ever agree a deal on the first meeting. I usually walk away with both sides feeling that they're at opposite ends of the spectrum. Perhaps we will end up agreeing not to agree. They might not sell the property to someone else, and I have kept the door open. Deals often come back because they think you're a decent person.

I was interested in buying a hotel in Europe. A few years ago I went in with an offer that was way below the seller's expectations. About six months ago they came back to me and asked if I was still interested in buying it. I gave them the same offer and they said, 'Still too low, but if you just come up a tiny little bit we'll do it.' I flew over to meet the council and everyone involved, and I raised the offer. I've also got an eighteen-month option to develop the site next door. The success came because I kept positive and left the door open and said to them, 'You know, we couldn't agree a price, but that's fine, if you ever want to do it again, you know where I am'... and they came back to me.

Generally, I don't do the hard-nosed negotiation act, but occasionally I bang my hand on the table at third parties saying, 'Get me the vendor, I want to speak to them, I'm not speaking to

> ## Rarely ever agree a deal on the first meeting

you any more.' I give the third party a really hard time and they think I'm a nightmare, and when I speak to the vendor he will be surprised that I'm a nice guy. That can be a useful tactic.

The importance of goodwill

Don't try to get blood out of a stone. The first real development property I bought was for £625,000 and I know I could have hammered the seller down to £600,000 or less, but I decided not to. I was getting a good deal at £625,000 and I did not want to push it any more. You can leave a little bit on the table for the guy that is already there. I'm happy with that deal and he's happy, too. I've left goodwill behind me. What goes around comes around, and you will find that people aren't as hardball with you. The guys I know who are really hardball, everyone else plays hardball with them. The guys I know who are a bit softer, everyone's a little bit softer. You've got to be ruthless, but you don't have to go for blood all the time.

> ## When there is good money on the table, always take it

Don't sweat the small stuff

No matter how big your deal is, don't sweat the pennies. People hold out for a couple of extra thousand, and end up losing good sales, simply because they're trying to get blood out of a deal. What's the point if you are getting a good deal? Take it, and if you feel you're getting a good deal, it's done. I have a friend who bought a property and refurbished it all in for £200,000, and had an offer on the table for £275,000. To me that's good money on the table. He was looking at £70,000 profit (after paying £5000 in estate agent and legal fees). But he wanted £285,000, so he did not take the offer. The market in the area has dropped and he'll be lucky to get £250,000. Greed hurts, and remember, when there is good money on the table, always take it.

6   Make the deal bigger

If someone is selling me a piece of land, will they sell me the piece of land next door? Always try and get more from your deal.

Just keep chipping away and making the deal better and better, and then at the end you may find you've got an amazing deal.

7 Closing the deal

You may have to move heaven and earth to close a deal. Patience is really important. Transactions may go on for days, so you have to learn to hold your nerve. Then again, a good friend of mine, one of the UK's biggest entrepreneurs, was buying a telecoms company in America. No one would agree the terms of the deal. He locked everyone in a room and wouldn't let them out until all the solicitors agreed all the points. He kept them in there for 24 hours until everything was agreed. All he gave them was water and coffee. That was it. No food. Everyone was shattered and wanted to sign just to get the thing over and done with. He walked away with the deal of the century. He is a very rich man, and knows exactly how to close deals. He is a genius!

8 Get your legal arrangements in order

When you have an agreement, it's important to document the details clearly. Once you walk away from the table, what the other person thinks you've agreed and what you think you've agreed are two separate things. I make a list of the agreed terms at the meeting and get the person to look at it and confirm that this is what we've agreed. This includes price, how price is structured, timescales, any bits and pieces that are in with the deal, deposits, legal issues, closing date, financial contingencies, and any further due diligence required. Then I send a confirming email on the day to make sure there's no ambiguity. When you write to people and they write back to you and confirm it, they find it very hard to backtrack.

Legal fees for property conveyancing are usually under £1,000 for buying one property, depending on how much legal work is involved. I recommend a fixed-fee arrangement with a solicitor because then you know your costs exactly. If the solicitor does a great job I give him or her a bonus.

Preparing and exchanging contracts

Once the deal is negotiated and agreed, contracts are prepared and exchanged. Your solicitor draws up the contract and you sign it. The seller signs an identical contract and your respective solicitors swap the signed documents in what is known as 'exchange of contracts'. The buyer usually has to pay a non-refundable deposit of 10 per cent

Get your full deposit

When selling, you are legally entitled to a deposit of 10 per cent from a buyer, but often buyers will try to put down less. If you accept less and they default, you have to go to court to get your full 10 per cent. It's always best to get it up front. The inverse is true. If you are buying, try to put down 5 per cent deposit or less. You are always trying to get the best possible deal for yourself. Your rules for what you would accept are different from what you want someone else to accept. That is how you make your money. I've had people pull out at the last minute because they couldn't get the rest of the money or couldn't get a mortgage. Then you have to start the sale all over again, but at least you keep the 10 per cent deposit.

Nothing is guaranteed until you have exchanged contracts. I've had sellers pull out on the day of exchange. When that happens you lose all the money you've spent on legal fees. For example, on a property I was selling, the buyer's mother visited the apartment on the day of exchange and decided she just didn't like it and they pulled out. It was a real kick in the teeth – but at the end of the day, that's property and you take the rough with the smooth.

❝ Nothing is guaranteed until you have exchanged contracts ❞

Risks between exchange and completion

You should insure the property that you're buying on exchange because legally you own that property, even though you haven't completed on it. When selling properties, I recommend you keep them insured in your name until the sale is complete.

Beware buyer's remorse

Have you ever been shopping and bought something quite expensive and got home and thought, 'Oh why in the hell did I buy that? Can I take it back, I've got to get it exchanged?' It's called 'buyer's remorse'. Once you've agreed the deal to sell something and you think you have got a great price, you need to close the deal as quickly as possible. The last thing you want is the buyer waking up next morning and deciding they have changed their minds. You don't want to risk buyer's remorse.

Gazumping and gazundering

Gazumping happens when there's a fast rising market and the demand for property is rising faster than the supply – i.e. there are more buyers than sellers. During negotiations the seller accepts a better offer before you exchange. Gazundering takes place in a falling market when the buyer drops the price just before exchange.

There was one deal that would have made me a million; it was a big piece of land on which I knew I could obtain planning permission. We had agreed to exchange contracts on a Friday. I'd already struck a deal with a housing association to buy it from me, subject to planning permission. I was confident about the planning permission because the precedents were set. I waited on the Friday for the exchange documents to come through. My solicitor called me and said, 'We still don't have anything.' I couldn't believe it. On Monday morning, I tried to get hold of the sellers – there was still no response. They'd been on the phone to me every twenty minutes up until the planned exchange day. Eventually I found out that they'd sold the property to another developer for fifty grand more. There was nothing we could do. So, always watch your back.

Special financial arrangements

One way to protect each investment when you are doing multiple deals is to set each purchase up within a single purpose vehicle, or 'SPV'. Because in law every company you set up is a separate legal entity, each SPV is a stand-alone project for each development. If you have difficulties with one development, it wouldn't affect the finance for any other SPVs that you have. Banks and developers like to use such vehicles and they're useful if you're entering partnerships or agreements with investors.

9 Completion

The contract you exchange will stipulate an agreed completion date. Simultaneous exchange and completion is possible, but a completion usually happens within two weeks of exchange. Another option is to negotiate a long stop or delayed completion. This is handy if you need time to gear up your workforce and get your materials in place. With a delayed completion of, say, three months, you know you've legally secured the property so you can start instructing builders. When you complete, your builders start on site on that day.

10 What not to do

Here are my top three tips for what *not* to do during negotiation. They are all classic beginner's mistakes:

- **Don't tell a potential buyer what's wrong with your property.** When you're selling you have to be honest, but you don't have to give everything away. Never appear desperate to sell. In negotiation, once somebody sniffs desperation they have a huge advantage over you, let them decide what they like and don't like. Keep it positive.

- **Don't get emotional.** Be clear about your price and timing, and don't get emotional about it. Don't fall in love with the deal. I go in with a philosophical attitude – if I get the deal, great, if I don't get it, there's always another one. There have been buildings that I wanted but find that I don't regret the deals that haven't been done. I just move on and find another one. There's always another deal round the corner.

- **Don't talk too much.** Silence is a powerful tool when you're negotiating. You don't want to give too much away and you want to find out information from the other side. Sometimes in the middle of negotiations you want to know if they want to do the deal or not. Here's a little trick I use sometimes: I'll say something like, 'Okay, I don't mean to be rude, but these are the terms I'd prefer to accept. This is your last chance. Do you want to do the deal or not?' And then I just stay silent and wait and see what they come back with. If they sense that you might be walking away you can tell really quickly what your position is.

So you've found the property that you want, you've done your due diligence; it's all looking so good! You've negotiated and closed on your life-changing deal. Now you've got to get the money to buy and finance your property. Apart from the question everyone asks me, 'How do you find the deals?' the next question I get asked most often is, 'How do you get the money to make it happen?' Follow me to the next chapter and I'll tell you.

10

Get your hands on the money

...financing your deal is easier than you think!

When I first started in property I went to four banks that blankly refused to lend me money. I had what I thought was a great business plan, a deal showing a healthy profit, and they just turned me down. Banks will sell you umbrellas in sunny weather, but when it starts raining they're nowhere to be seen. In other words, in the good times you can get as much money as you want, but in the bad times, like now, when you need them to help you, they're not there. If you look at any businessman who's been hugely successful, you'll find that banks have turned most of them down at one time or another. Don't be disheartened.

There was a time when the supply of money seemed to be endless. Well, that's not the case anymore. This is now one of your biggest challenges – 'finding the finance' – and isn't going to get any easier.

1. Finding a great deal is harder than finding capital
2. Understand mortgages: take advice from an independent financial advisor
3. Understand financing and debt
4. How to work with private investors and joint ventures
5. Other financing options
6. Buy – add value – sell FAST

Remember that according to the entrepreneur Felix Dennis there are only six ways of obtaining capital:

1. You can be given it or inherit it
2. You can win it
3. You can marry it
4. You can steal it
5. You can earn it
6. You can borrow it

If you're hoping to get money by 1, 2 or 3 remember – your elderly aunt can always leave her money to the cats' home, your chance of dying on your way to buy your lottery ticket is probably greater than your chance of winning the jackpot, and divorces cost money. If you've already got the money through methods 1, 2 or 3, good luck to you – you've got your equity so now you can start building your empire.

If you haven't got the money yet that leaves the other three methods. Stealing isn't recommended, as you will probably get caught. I've found that honesty is the best policy and that you reap what you sow – being an honest and decent person is much more important than becoming rich. So we're down to two, earning and borrowing. Earning money is the way to get your initial equity, and borrowing is the way to make huge amounts of money, whether it is from investors, partners, banks or mortgages. You've got to earn a certain amount to get yourself started, but the future is all about borrowing.

1 Finding a great deal is harder than finding capital

This certainly used to be the case, but I still think it holds true. Remember, getting the money isn't the hardest part of property development. Getting great deals is harder than finding money, because if you've found a great deal, there are plenty of people who will back you. For example, if you go to a bank or an investor with a plot of land that should have cost a million but you bought it for £300,000, and you can clearly show why it's worth a million and why you're getting it so cheaply, you're going to get a lot of people who'll say, 'Okay, I'll give you the money.' What is better is that you don't have to put a penny into the deal yourself because the deal is so good. The investors will be lining up. It happens all the time.

2 Understand mortgages

If you are starting from zero, your best way to get on the property market is via a mortgage. The great thing about property is that banks like it more than other business opportunities. Uniquely, unlike a business based on cash flow, property is an asset, and property prices, on average, go up every year.

Forget bank debt or bank loans at the early stage of your property development career; banks are a totally different type of financer and are more stringent. Always remember: banks don't take risks – you do. Mortgages mean you don't have to earn a great deal to receive the equity to get your business started. So, without doubt, for your first few steps getting started in property, you should get a mortgage.

Mortgage companies lend you money to borrow against the property that you're going to buy and live in, for buy-to-let development schemes, and for improving properties. You can borrow against the property, but the credit crunch has made things much harder and 100 per cent mortgages are now a thing of the past. Obviously, if the mortgage company lends close to what the property's worth, the terms become worse than if you can put a bigger deposit down. But a mortgage is an easy way to get into the property market with minimum cash.

I advise people to have at least a 10 per cent deposit, so if you're buying a property costing £100,000, you need £10,000 to get you started. The larger your deposit, the better chance you have of getting mortgage deals and terms that work for you.

There are two parts to the mortgage equation: your equity, which is the money that you already have (the cash you put into the deal) and your loan, which is the mortgage.

There are many types of mortgage. To find the type that suits you it is probably worth seeing an independent financial adviser. They usually have a software package that will input all your details and come up with a mortgage that best suits your situation. Look for a mortgage that you can get out of without any penalties. As a property developer you are going to develop the property and sell it on as soon as you can, so you will need a mortgage that you can set up and then leave as cheaply as possible. Sometimes that might mean paying a slightly higher interest rate. This is much more challenging than it used to be, but there are still options available:

£ **Interest-only mortgage.** Monthly payments will only cover the interest on the loan taken out with the lender. The full amount needs to be repaid by the end of the loan term. Most people invest additional money each month into a savings vehicle (i.e. endowment or ISA policy) in the expectation that it will grow and eventually pay off the mortgage.

£ **Repayment mortgage:** Monthly repayments repay some of the capital along with the interest on the loan.

£ **Fixed-rate mortgage.** The interest rate is set for a set period of time (usually between one and five years). After that period, the rate returns to variable rate. This is a very competitive mortgage that provides protection against interest rate fluctuations.

However, there can be high set-up fees and tied deals with redemption penalties are common. Often these are the best option in volatile interest markets, and if you're investing in property to rent out, a fixed rate mortgage is excellent because you know exactly how much you have to repay every month for the number of years you plan to rent.

£ **Discounted mortgage.** The interest rate margin is set at a margin below the standard variable rate. You may get huge interest rate discounts in the short-term, which can be perfect if you want to develop and sell property quickly with minimum outlay. However, there are usually redemption penalties, and if interest rates increase, you pay more.

£ **Capped-rate mortgage.** This has a fixed upper rate, i.e. if rates are increasing, you are protected, if rates fall you can take advantage of the interest rate coming down. Deals are not the most competitive.

£ **Base rate tracker mortgage.** Tracks the Bank of England's base rate and changes in accordance with a constant differential set by the lender. At the mercy of the Bank of England's monetary committee who meet on the first Thursday of every month to decide what to do with the base rate.

£ **100 per cent mortgage:** You can borrow the complete cost of the purchase of the property, so there is no need for a deposit and if the market rises in the first year then you have accrued some equity. However, interest rates are high and the number of deals available is now extremely limited – I don't think we'll see these again.

£ **Flexible mortgage.** Allows flexibility for you to pay the mortgage weekly, take payment holidays, and take withdrawals as the property goes up in value. If you are developing a property and your cash flow runs out, a flexible mortgage allows you a 'holiday' from payments. It's a way of hedging your bets if something goes wrong; you've got a little bit of leniency to let you recover.

£ **Developing mortgage.** A relatively new mortgage that allows you to borrow the full cost to buy the property, together with funds for renovations or extension based on the projected sale price. This is a hybrid-type mortgage, and appeals to first-time property developers. If you can find this type of deal it might work better for you, especially when you're just starting out and you need every penny you can get, but I think they are a thing of the past.

> **When you are in business, debt isn't necessarily a bad thing** ""

3 Understand financing and debt

It is possible to borrow from a bank but as well as having a strong, detailed business plan, you will need to show a good track record and a good credit history. You also need to be able to put up some of your own money – something many new property developers cannot do. Banks will expect 25 to 35 per cent deposits before they will let you borrow the rest, while on a mortgage you can borrow 95 per cent of your property value.

Before you approach the bank you will need to provide as much as possible from the following list:

- Detailed business plan

- Cash flow spreadsheet

- Show that the deal can make 25 per cent + return on capital

- Track record of success

- Equity/capital (usually 30 per cent of the total costs)

- Personal guarantee

- Personal commitment

As I mentioned earlier, when I wanted to start my first property development I put a business plan together and visited four different high street banks. They all rejected me. I had built up a couple of hundred thousand pounds but it wasn't enough because the deal was for a million-pound development. The banks wanted to see a track record and I didn't have one. They wanted to see a bigger deposit. It was a Catch-22 situation – I found it really frustrating. To get around the problem, I found a business partner. A builder agreed to come in 50/50 with me in a company. He'd been building for 30 years and he had a good track record with the banks. We both put up our money and the bank was happy to lend us what we needed.

Debt

There are a lot of different categories of what you'd call 'debt'. People hear the word 'debt' and they go white, but when you're in business, debt isn't necessarily a bad thing. If you buy a coat it immediately becomes a depreciating asset that will be worth less after you've bought it and worn it. But in property a debt is just money you are leveraging against assets. So, technically that debt is always secure.

The more debt you can raise, the bigger projects you can potentially take on. If you can borrow £10m for a scheme because you are expecting a 20 per cent return, then you should be able to make £2m profit. The more you borrow, the more money you can make. If you borrow £100m you should make £20m. The more debts you have against properly secured assets, potentially the more profits you will make. It goes against rational thinking, but in property developing debt can be good. So all developers are trying to leverage themselves up as much as possible (within reason).

What the banks will lend you

Depending on how good your deal is, your track record, how much cash you have to put into the project or indeed how good your business plan is, here is a guide to what banks should be prepared to lend you. It also shows you how you can finance a large project, rather than relying on your own money. Remember, if things go wrong, you will always lose your money first. Banks have what is called a 'first charge' on everything borrowed, which means they get their money back first and you are usually at the very end of the queue. You are the fall guy. If the wheels fall off, you are the one who loses everything and gets left high and dry.

65–70 per cent Senior loan: Usually from a major high street bank that expects a 5–10 per cent return and usually charges 1.5 per cent to 5 per cent above the Bank of England base rate. If the property is repossessed, they will be the first partner to reclaim their investment after it has been sold.

10–20 per cent Mezzanine loan: A further loan usually from a specialist property lender (sometimes called a boutique bank) that will look to make 5–15 per cent above the Bank of England base rate. The rate varies depending on how risky they see the loan. This bank has the next claim on any proceeds from the sale of the property.

5 per cent Partner/Investor: This sits above the Senior and Mezzanine debt and will probably want to turn at least a 20 per cent profit, if not take a larger slice of the profits, in exchange for the risk. If the market drops just 10 per cent, or you overspend, they lose their money.

5–10 per cent Your own equity: If the market drops just 5 or 10 per cent, or your costs overrun so that the project makes a loss, you will take the hit, insulating everyone below you.

Partnership: Some banks will enter into equity financing where they effectively become your partner and take a stake in the project, but as usual, expect to be the fall guy in the project.

4 How to work with private investors and joint ventures

Most financial institutions require a borrower to personally guarantee every loan and to comply with very stringent credit and paperwork requirements. This is why many people turn to partners or private investors who lend on property without personal guarantees. Private investment is a way of getting equity to help you borrow money from the bank. A private investor is someone who lends you money looking for a percentage return on their money each year plus a share of the profits. If they give you all the equity that you need, they might want 60 per cent of the profits. If they give you a part of the equity that you need, they might want 20 per cent, although it is negotiable. Relatives, friends, employers, and business acquaintances may all be good sources of money but they will want a good return.

I try to take on investors and partners for specific transactions only – property by property or deal by deal. Always use a solicitor and draw up a formal contract with a clear exit strategy. It makes sense to set up a SPV (Special Purpose Vehicle, see page 125) for every transaction to ring-fence every deal.

Business angels

These are wealthy individuals or private investors who are prepared to take a risk on you and provide the cash for your project. If you don't know where to find someone like this you'll need to start networking with accountants, lawyers, retirees, investment advisors, business support agencies, suppliers and others. They will invest money in your scheme for a percentage of the business, or a profit share. They are called 'angels' because they give you cash and there's no recourse on that cash. If you take money off your family or friends and you end up losing it, it puts a huge strain on your personal relationships – a business angel is a better idea.

> **If you take money off your family and you end up losing it, you'll never hear the end of it**

Joint ventures with a vendor

Sometimes the person who is selling the plot of land or the building will work with you to develop and sell their property and share the profits. In a joint venture with a vendor, you can arrange a deal without having to buy the land. In my experience this is a hard sell because the vendor always wants more than their share is actually worth, although I have known it to work, especially in larger schemes. Large companies will join forces to do a deal where someone puts in the land and the other person develops it. For example, on a development on the banks of the Thames, Thames Water put in the land, and Berkeley's Homes did the development. They shared the proceeds when the development was sold.

Buying from developers or 'off-plan' means buying a property that has yet to be built. Often, developers will settle for a 10 per cent deposit. You get to share the market risk (i.e. if the market drops you take the hit) but you may also benefit from the deal, without vast outlay. Developers are often keen to give huge discounts (5–20 per cent). The reasons they can do this are that they are developing in bulk and so have economies of scale, and it de-risks the project for the developer, and, of course, the 10 per cent deposit helps with their cash flow.

Many developers and block sellers offer excellent incentive packages including 5 per cent cash back, payment of Stamp Duty, payment of solicitors fees, up-grade of fixtures and fittings and quite often they can provide a mortgage company that is willing to finance on the terms they offer. When the property is finished you can either rent or sell. But beware! This works well in a rising market, but could seriously backfire in a falling market.

5 Other financing options

There are always new methods of finding the money, so long as you have the life-changing deal in your hands. Proceed with caution if you need to go to a finance company, as they often charge extortionate interest rates, and it is easy to get in over your head. You could also consider:

Government Grants (DTI Loans). In certain areas you can get government grants to renovate and refurbish properties in run-down areas. You can also apply for a DTI loan to start up a new business that the government will guarantee.

Credit cards. You can use a credit card to borrow money. Interest rates are huge, however, but you may have a great deal that it could work for. Just take it from me that this is not recommended . . . but I have to admit that I have done it in the past! Take my advice; don't copy me.

Second mortgage. This can be a good way to raise funds to buy a property. The term of the loan is shorter, so payments could be larger. It is usually only allowed under FSA regulations for holiday homes.

The key thing to remember is that markets go up and down. As a property developer you must always add value to your properties, so that if the market falls, you have better equity return. If interest rates keep going up and the market starts going down, those who have a lot of debt against their assets will have problems.

6 Buy – add value – sell FAST

Property developing is safest when you get in and out quickly. My rule is: Buy – add value – sell FAST. Even in a falling market you can make money by adding value to your development. However, long-term, property does go up by, on average, 10 per cent a year. As long as you can see any development through the bad times, the good times will come back.

Any multi-millionaire will tell you that earning the first million is the hardest, and so it is. You can take heart from the fact that most developers start from almost nothing. If they can, so can you! Getting your first scheme off the ground is a killer. You've got to beg and borrow (but not steal!) to get yourself going. But you can take heart from the thought that most developers start from almost nothing. If they can do it, you can too. And remember, you're never too old to do this – the thing about property development is that you can start it any time.

Now you've got your deal, and you've (hopefully) got your money, let's work out what you're going to do next. Let's make sure your life-changing deal reaches its full potential. You've got to get your specification right for your target market because, believe me, first impressions count!

First impressions

...always stand out from the crowd!

When I first started in property I was building and refurbishing apartments, and I didn't put flooring in. My theory that people would want to choose their own flooring was wrong, because the apartments looked unfinished. None of the properties sold. I put oak flooring into the hall and living rooms, beautiful ceramic tiling in the kitchens, and neutral carpets in the bedrooms. Within 24 hours the offers came flooding in. It is a sad fact that most people do not have the imagination to see how something might be – if it is not in front of their eyes, it is hard to convince them.

When I was doing bigger developments, I'd put together a show house, because first impressions count. The better you can make something look, the more chance you have of selling it quickly and getting the best possible price. That's what this game's all about – providing a great product and reaping the rewards. Here are the essential elements to make sure you present your property to its full potential:

1. Write a specification: only include ideas that will help sell the property
2. Know your market: tailor your specification to it
3. Create a great first impression
4. Keep décor plain and simple
5. Buy the worst property and make it the best
6. Provide great kitchens and bathrooms: these are central to your selling strategy
7. Go for a high-quality finish
8. Don't forget outside spaces
9. Take environmental issues seriously: good for the planet and add value to your property

1 Write a specification

The purpose of a specification is to sell your property to its full potential. List what you plan to do, down to the smallest detail. Only include something that will attract the buyers and add value to your development. If you don't stick to a written specification, you might do or buy things on a whim because you like the look of it. Everything in your specification should help you get the highest price for your property, as quickly as possible. You can use a specification to brief your builder or contractor.

2 Know your market

Think about whom you plan to sell to. You have read about this in the earlier chapters, but now you are going to act on your information. Your specification will depend on whether you are selling to a family, a student, a newly married couple, or a city executive. Don't let your own emotions get in the way – you're not the buyer. On many of the TV shows that I've presented the contributors make the same mistake. They introduce bold prints, paint the walls strong colours, and choose strange bathrooms and kitchens. That is not the way to sell a property. Find the right lifestyle buttons to push. If students will buy or rent your property, put in a very basic kitchen because you know it's probably going to get trashed. If you have a clear idea of whom you are selling to, it will be easier to write a good specification.

" **Everything in your specification should help you get the highest price for your property** "

You need to please your potential customers. I had a penthouse flat that I wanted to sell for £350,000, which was quite expensive for the area. A woman saw it and said, 'I'll buy the flat off you today if you give me a pink Smeg fridge.' There was already a silver Smeg fridge, which looked really good, but she wanted a pink one. I immediately said, 'Fine, I'll give you a pink Smeg fridge,' and she did the deal. It didn't cost me much, and when I met her two years later she said, 'Oh I love the apartment, and thank you so much for the pink Smeg fridge.' Just by tweaking the spec for her, I had a happy customer.

3 Create a great first impression

I always like to create the 'wow' factor when people view my properties, but the type of impression you will create depends on the market you are aiming for. I develop at the higher end of the market (£250,000+), so my specifications are always top-notch. But whatever your market you need to start off with the entrance.

A reporter asked me to look at her flat in Central London and tell her how she could sell it, and where she was going wrong. It was immediately obvious. At the front of the building there were bins and rubbish lying around and a bit of unkempt garden full of weeds. The paintwork was crumbling and the tiles were broken. The first impression was so bad I didn't want to go in. It got worse. In the communal entrance there was a horrible old carpet and bare light bulbs. It hadn't been painted in years and there was a nasty smell. The apartment itself was really pleasant but it was too late; the damage had been done. The first impression is vital – people can be put off immediately.

> **The number one way to sell property is to have excellent 'kerb appeal'**

Make sure your entrance is clean and tidy. Research shows that the colour of your front door can help you sell your house for more. Black, dark blue and deep red are the colours that sell. Add good-quality door furniture. Put a really nice chandelier in the hallway, and you're halfway there.

Anne Maurice, the 'House Doctor', says the number one way to sell a property is to have excellent 'kerb appeal'. The exterior of the property is really important. Make sure you have good windows and windowsills, and add attractive, good-quality plants.

4 Keep décor plain and simple

My advice is to keep the inside simple. I always choose neutral colour schemes. My walls are usually painted in Dulux's 'Timeless White' in soft sheen in every room. This makes the walls look smoother and reflects the light really well. I use a pure brilliant white paint on the ceiling; this reflects down to create a really spacious bright feel. I paint the skirting boards and doorframes eggshell white (this gives a matt finish). Radiators are also white.

I put laminate oak floors in the hall, living room and kitchens (usually with a tiled area as well). I run the oak flooring the length of the room, not across it, because it makes the room feel longer. In the bedrooms I put a reasonable quality wool and polyester mix carpet in a neutral colour such as straw. Spotlights rather than lampshades keeps the lighting bright, simple and not fussy.

> **I like to give people a blank canvas to do what they want**

Everything is designed to create light and space and people seem to love it. I like to give people a blank canvas to do what they want. It might seem bland but if you start putting colour in, which I occasionally do, it can put people off. They can get emotional about colours. You paint a wall red and you think it looks really cool and then you get people coming who hate the red wall and immediately begin to have negative thoughts. You don't want them to be talking about anything they don't like – if you keep things neutral there's nothing for them to take a dislike to.

I like the finish and fittings to be smart because that's the kind of market I'm going for. Even at the lower end of the market it is best to keep things neutral and light. When I first started development, I found places that were absolutely awful – brown curtains, horrible carpet, terrible wallpaper and no natural light. I would put laminate floors in, paint the place white, change the curtains to blinds, and generally open it up and let as much light in as possible. You can do that in a week, and it looks like a totally different property.

5 Buy the worst property and make it the best

I've said it before but it's worth repeating: you should always buy the worst house in the best street. Buy something in a street that's on the up, and then try to make it the best property in that street. That's the way you'll make maximum money. I always try to make my house slightly different and more valuable than anything else in the same street. Look at what your neighbours are doing, and then make your property stand out by giving it a unique selling point ('USP'). There are many ways to do this but you have to be creative.

Create light and space

One of the properties I bought had private access to a roof – a wonky ladder up to a horrible roof that no one had looked at for years. I put in a cool, funky ladder (it was still a ladder, but it was safe and sexy), and I cleaned up the roof. I added a table and chairs and some plants, and made a little oasis on the top of the flat. That added a huge amount of value. In another property, I added a Velux skylight, which let the light stream in. Again, it added value. Yet no one else had done these things.

I don't put ceilings in the upstairs of new-build properties if I can help it. I open the space right to the top of the roof and put a couple of big skylights in – the light streams in, creating a cathedral-effect. This works in the entrance and in the bedrooms, although there might be times when you want to maximise space by having extra bedrooms up there.

Natural light is one of your biggest selling points. In an experiment, children were allowed to play where they liked in a large hall. Part of the hall was lit artificially, and two areas were lit by sunshine. All the children preferred the sunlit areas, even though the rest of the hall was lit just as brightly. Maximising your daylight gives a feel-good factor, as well as making your property seem larger. You can do this by making sure the windows are not restricted by curtains, that they are clean, and that the walls are in a light colour; and, of course, you can enhance the light using mirrors.

> " Maximising your daylight gives a feel-good factor, as well as making your property seem larger "

Change the layout and room count

I think most people don't really understand how layout should work. In every single development, even though architects design them, I go over all the layouts again and usually change them. It's annoying because the architects have done so much work on them, but it's worth it when people say: 'Wow, this is so cool.' Usually the best way to get this reaction is to take walls down. I always try to take walls down between halls and living rooms so you immediately enter a huge living room with lots of light and space; it feels twice as big.

> " Keep it really simple with uncluttered worktops "

However, it won't work in every development. Once again, consider your market. How many rooms do your buyers want? For some people it is more important to have more rooms than lots of open space. Someone with children is probably going to want several small bedrooms rather than one or two big ones. I design kitchens so that we can sell it as open plan, but people can put up a stud wall to divide it if they want. And where does a family keep the coats if you get rid of the hall? Try and think of a solution. Add a garden shed for bikes, and coats can go in a downstairs cloakroom.

6 Provide great kitchens and bathrooms

Kitchens and bathrooms are central to your selling strategy. They're the two big things that people look out for. People spend a lot of time in the kitchen and the bathroom and they want those to be places that stand out.

Your kitchen doesn't have to be top of the range, but a good-quality kitchen, such as Bulthaup, is attractive. You can get a perfectly good kitchen from somewhere like MFI or Homebase; they'll design a great kitchen for you. They can advise you on tiles and worktops and you really just have to pick what you think your market, your buyer, will be interested in.

There are many choices, but keep it really simple with uncluttered worktops. Plain Shaker-style doors are neat and simple. It is essential to fit kitchen appliances – people expect them and when buyers are looking round it looks much better to have all the equipment in place. You need to show there is space for a dishwasher and washing machine. In the grand scheme of things, appliances aren't that expensive.

For bathrooms, a ceramic-tiled floor in a neutral colour like sandstone or off white, with a Philippe Starck shower and bath looks good. People notice good bathroom fittings these days. A really good shower system is another selling point. Spotlights and lots of mirrors make a bathroom feel spacious.

7 Go for a high-quality finish

The quality of the overall finish makes a big difference to your sale. Buyers are discerning and they want things finished to the highest standard. I received about a dozen emails from a buyer because a plug socket was crooked in one of the apartments I'd sold. Another time, one of the developers on a TV show did a rush job to get a house sold. It made a great first impression, but as so often happens, the potential buyers came back for a second look, but on this visit the rose-tinted glasses came off. Once they looked at the house carefully they could see there was paint on the radiators, the cooker was damaged, the floorboards were creaky.

> **Buyers are discerning and they want things finished to the highest standard**

To get those finishes right wouldn't have cost much more; it was just a matter of attention to detail.

I always like to make sure that anything someone can touch is really good quality. One thing that people always do when they're looking round is open and close the doors. I fit good door handles so that potential buyers feel they are buying something strong and solid. A solid door feels more substantial and better quality when you open it than a cheaper hollow door.

Soundproofing

Great soundproofing is a huge selling point and I draw attention to it in my brochures. In a recent development on a noisy road I installed triple-glazed soundproofed windows at the front of the house and now inside the properties you can hear a pin drop. The windows had small vents that can be opened to let in some air, but prevent the noise. They're a little more expensive but the peace and quiet is a big plus.

Building regulations (see page 161) are quite strong on soundproofing. The regulations constantly change; for example, they allow a maximum of 62 decibels or less for a new build and 64 decibels or less for a conversion, but a normal timber floor transmits 75 decibels, and therefore requires soundproofing. I usually put in extra soundproofing between flats. Before you buy a property in an old building ask a few questions to find out if there are noisy neighbours; avoid it if there are.

If you install wooden floors, add soundproof mats first. Not only will you not hear the people below, they won't hear you and complain.

Underfloor heating

Where possible I put in underfloor heating, which avoids having intrusive radiators everywhere. Once the underfloor heating reaches the temperature that you set, it maintains a constant temperature, and you never have to turn the heat up or down. Research has shown that people feel comfortable at 21 degrees. Bedrooms need to be cooler for sleep – say 18 degrees. Underfloor heating is a bit more expensive than radiators, but it's a more sophisticated way forward in heating systems. However, as well as having underfloor heating, I install chrome towel radiators in bathrooms that can be turned on and off when required.

Air-conditioning

At the higher end of the market, air-conditioning and comfort cooling is expected now, especially in major cities. However, it is environmentally unsound. An effective alternative is to insert a louvre system in windows, with vents at the top and bottom of a window. Air-conditioning may be considered essential in city apartments.

8 Don't forget outside spaces

Outside space is very important to buyers. I try to put in at least a balcony in every single development I do. Balconies are always well received. A Juliet balcony is very shallow, sometimes only inches deep, straight across a window, but it means you can install floor-to-ceiling windows. It's a great way to add more light and increase airflow and it gives an opulent feel.

Decking is going out of fashion now, because, apart from the fact that it has become a bit of a cliché, if food drops between the decking planks, it rots, smells and attracts vermin. If you choose to lay decking, place the wood really close together to avoid gaps. Tiled and paved areas seem to be making a comeback.

Landscaping

Landscaping is a hugely important selling feature. The buyer will be thinking, 'Can I entertain my friends out here?' or 'Will it impress my new girlfriend/boyfriend?' If you plan to sell to a family they will need to see that the garden is suitable for children. But don't forget that family buyers will also be asking, 'What do my friends think?' and so the landscaping has to create the right environment to satisfy these demands.

" If you have space, put in a parking space "

Parking

These days councils are encouraging car-free property development schemes.

But that's nonsense. There's no such thing as car-free – people own cars, and they've got to park them somewhere. Councils are just passing the problem on to somewhere else. I try to incorporate parking in my developments. If you have space, put in a parking space. If your development is right next to a tube or bus station, and your market is a commuter, parking may not be essential.

9 Take environmental issues seriously

The environmental efficiency of buildings is important. I think it is our duty to build things that are energy efficient. Every household in the UK creates around six tonnes of carbon dioxide (CO_2) every year, so by creating buildings that are self-sustaining or carbon neutral we can help the environment. Buildings last for hundreds of years and if you build them with environment-friendly features, you are doing some good for the planet. Creating environment-friendly buildings is also very advantageous to the property developer:

- There is no Stamp Duty to pay when buying a zero-emission home, until 2012.

- There are discounts and grants for putting in turbines, solar panels and deep-ground heaters.

- It adds value to your development. In Britain, 63 per cent of adults said they would pay more for an energy-efficient home. The average household could save up to £250 a year on energy bills through energy efficiency.

Easy ways to make your development 'green'

Here are some things you can do to help reduce your carbon footprint and boost your profits:

Reflect heat. Put aluminium foil reflectors behind radiators to direct heat back into the room. Keep furniture away from radiators to allow heat to circulate.

Switch to energy-saving light bulbs. They last around ten times longer and could save up to £60 on electricity over the bulb's lifetime.

Get glazing. Cover your windows with a solar reflective film as it reflects heat in the summer to keep you cool and keeps out the cold during winter.

Update your boiler. Over £2 billion is wasted on energy in the UK every year due to out-of-date central heating systems. New condensing boilers can cut power bills by a third and save around one tonne of CO_2 a year.

Insulate. By installing cavity wall insulation, the average house could reduce heating costs by 15 per cent and save around one tonne of CO_2 a year.

Stop draughts. Fill gaps under skirting boards and between floorboards with beading or sealant.

Swap your bath for a shower. Increasingly, they are more popular with buyers, and waste a lot less water and energy when heating the water.

Think solar panels, wind turbines or hydro power. Generating your own electricity will give your home a higher score for its Energy Performance Certificate, and you will have a great talking point that could make you money when you sell the property. If you generate more than you use, it is also possible to sell the extra energy back to the National Grid! Solar Thermal Hot Water systems can supply around 50–70 per cent of your hot water for free, and can add up to £10,000 to your property price.

Use natural building materials. You can use natural material like earth, straw bale, cob, and other varieties of ecological building materials to improve indoor air quality, eliminate toxic chemicals, and create a healthier building.

Natural landscaping. Good landscaping enhances sunlight, water and air, and adds to the aesthetics of the building. Selecting the right plants and soil can reduce landscape maintenance costs and noise pollution, and encourage birds and wildlife.

Project-manage
your site

...roll up your sleeves and get stuck
in, it's the best way to learn!

I'm not going to beat around the bush here. Managing
a development is an absolute nightmare. You need to have
military organisation, you need to be diligent, you need to
work night and day, and you've got to motivate teams of
people. You've got to pull together the whole project like
some huge jigsaw and most of the time the pieces don't fit.
You have to find solutions to any problems that arise.

You are responsible for bringing the project in on time, to the specification you want and, most importantly, within budget. But don't let me put you off. If you really want to make that million then grit your teeth and use this chapter to find the best way of managing your project. Here are your project management essential elements:

1 Get your hands dirty

2 Find the right contractors: get written quotes from at least three builders

3 Use contracts: fixed price is the best way to control your costs

4 Write a clear specification: leave no room for ambiguity

5 Keep on top of things: have a detailed schedule and a back-up builder

1 Get your hands dirty

Most developers start by getting their hands dirty, and this is useful when you become a project manager. I have spent many hours scraping woodchip off walls. I've done papering, I've laid floors, I've fitted doors, I've painted a whole house – you name it, I've probably done it. It's a great way to learn what materials cost, what labour costs, and how the whole house or apartment is put together. Even when I go to meetings to talk about multi-million-pound contracts, I know how much pipes and paint cost – I have my feet on the ground. Some experienced developers will continue to be their own project managers.

If you are starting out you may have no choice but to do the work yourself, and certainly to project-manage it yourself. The exception is plumbing and electrics; always get an expert to do them.

❝ Stay focused, know the market, and stick to your original concept ❞ If you are project managing, you have to understand the schedule of work that needs to be done. The problem is that a lot of people get carried away – once the work is underway they keep getting 'good ideas' – these invariably add to the costs. You have to stay focused, know the market, and stick to your original concept and schedule.

2 Find the right contractors

Having a good builder or main contractor is essential to the smooth and swift running of any project, and most importantly, ensures you protect your profit margin. Yet finding a good builder is difficult. Builders and other tradesmen are notoriously bad timekeepers and frequently let you down. It's probably because they're their own boss; they don't have to report to anyone and if they don't want to turn up, they won't. There's such a shortage of good people to do this work that people have little choice in who they use, but once you have found a good one, treat them well so they will work for you again.

How do you find a good builder?

Recommendations are the best route. Ask your friends and neighbours, and keep a record of who did what. You may not need that person straight away, but you may in the future. You can also find one yourself. If you're ever passing a building site, and it looks as if the builders are doing a great job, just pop in and introduce yourself. Ask them if they've got anyone available to work with you. It's a useful way to find tradespeople, because you can look at their work and see them working at first hand.

> **Always get written quotes from a minimum of three different builders so you can compare them**

Last year rogue builders conned UK homeowners out of £1.3 billion. To avoid this, always get written quotes from a minimum of three different builders so you can compare them. Ask them to itemise everything. Good builders will always make an effort to explain exactly how much materials cost and how much labour is involved. And they won't be afraid to tell you how much they're making from a job. You need to find people who can do the work you need quickly, professionally, within budget, and to the specification you want.

In a new-build scheme it might take a contractor six weeks to give you a costing. If it is a small project you might have a quote right away, or at most, within two weeks. My advice is always to have a back-up. If your builder lets you down, get someone else in right away to ensure your project doesn't fall behind schedule.

3 Use contracts

You need a contract with your main contractor or builder, and the more complex the project, the more complex the contract. You can download sample contracts from the Federation of Master Builders and the National House Building Council, but a contract needs to cover:

- Quality of work and specifications

- Price, with each component itemised

- Timescales – build in payment penalties for late delivery

- Schedule of works

- Responsibilities of the builder

- Insurance that work will be carried out in accordance with Building Regulations

Remember to hold back about 10 per cent of the payment until all the final details (snags) are complete.

Fixed price contracts

I like to negotiate a fixed price budget with builders, but it is important to agree a really detailed specification of the work with them. Fixed price means that if it goes over time, it's their time, and if they've charged too low a price it is their problem. The builders are always going to be motivated with fixed price, as they'll want to get off site and get their money as quickly as they can. You will make it clear you're not paying a penny more than the price you have agreed unless they've really got a reason you can accept. For example, once they start ripping out the kitchen they might say that there's a huge plumbing issue that they haven't budgeted for. If you're in any doubt about a builder's claim that he needs more money for something, get a second opinion from another builder.

4 Write a clear specification

You have to be very, very clear with your builder about what you want them to do. This must all be laid out in the specification you draw up, including the type of materials you want. I usually source the materials I want myself to ensure quality fittings. Remember, if you don't tell them what you want, builders will just go and do whatever it takes to get the job done. For example, if you don't explain clearly where you want radiators, they'll put them wherever they feel like. If you don't explain clearly what kind of beading, paint, or finish you want on the walls, they will choose their own. If you don't explain clearly the way you want your kitchen, they'll do it the way they want to build it. When you communicate with builders, you've got to make what it is you want, absolutely crystal clear at the outset, with no room whatsoever for ambiguity.

In today's market, you've got to be very particular because buyers have high expectations. For example, I was building a block of flats, each with a megaflow system (a pressurised hot water cylinder that provides a power shower). The flats were tiny one-bedroom apartments, so I left instructions to put the first megaflow in the corner of the kitchen and I went away for a couple of days. When I came back the builders had put it where the fridge was meant to be. They had rerouted all the pipes, and built a wall, and then put the megaflow in the worst possible location. That mistake cost me £10,000. It was too much of a nightmare to rip it down, to redo all the plumbing, and to re-plaster, so I had to take a reduction in the final sale price of the apartment. Ultimately, it was my fault as I didn't make my instructions clear enough in the first place.You can have some crazy rows with builders, but you don't want to fall out with them – if you get a builder that's half decent, you've got to keep them on side.

5 Keep on top of things

It is crucial to the success of your project to be very organised and keep clear records of every stage. It helps you to get a smooth project out of potential chaos.

- **Keep a close eye on every penny you're spending.** Keep all your invoices, because when you sell your property, you will need to show what it cost when you file your tax return.

- **Prepare a giant chart to plot the timescale of your project.** Your chart should show you what activity should be going on in every single week slot, virtually to the day, and then you can see instantly if you've fallen behind. The chart will help you plot how well you're doing against your timescale and your budget.

- **Source materials yourself.** You've got to be particular in the look you want, and to make that happen, it is probably better to source the materials yourself. Put them on site for the builder to use in time for when they need them. If you do let the main contractor do any sourcing, be very specific about what you want. Work hard at sourcing materials, but don't forget the familiar big stores – Homebase, B&Q, MFI, Habitat and Ikea all have more than enough great materials, at reasonable prices.

- **Keep an eye on the specification.** This is one of the most enjoyable elements of property development. But never forget that your job as project manager is to think about your buyer. Keep your own emotions out of the project. It doesn't matter what your personal style is – you're not going to live there.

Now, as your company grows and your projects become bigger you will find that you need to delegate. This is a point where you need to start outsourcing – Richard Branson doesn't know how to fly jumbo jets; he employs people who can fly them for him. I don't know how to pour huge foundations; I employ companies that are experts and have created foundations for dozens of years. You too need to start creating what I call a wealth team to help you grow your business. The next chapter shows you how to do it.

13

Build your wealth team

...it's all about working with great people!

Growing a business is all about the people. People who are experts in their field will make your life easier. They help you get projects, bring projects in on time, on budget, and to the specification you want. They free up my time so I can focus on what's really important – finding deals and getting them financed.

You will be doing your own project management when you first get started, then as quickly as you can, you should outsource this to your wealth team. So who makes up the 'wealth team'? Who are these people that will help you get to the next level? Here are the essentials:

1 Use a strong team of professionals: working with an architect, structural engineer, quantity surveyor, landscape designer and project manager

2 Work in harmony: manage disputes and use your team to reach a solution

3 Work with the Building Regulations department (not the same as planning permission)

1 Use a strong team of professionals

A serious property developer working on big projects needs a project team. Although you can do project management yourself and save money by liaising with architects, builders, plumbers and electricians, and putting together your own contract, this isn't a good idea in the long run. As the business grows you will need the support of experienced professionals.

If banks are lending you money, they will expect you to use reliable professionals – you're not running a 'Mickey Mouse' outfit. Not everyone who reads this book will end up constructing hundreds of apartments and houses, but I hope some of you will. So you will need to have a strong chain of professionals you can rely on. In this chapter I look at the roles and responsibilities of each link in this chain to give you a clear idea of every discipline involved in a big project.

The architect

Responsible for designing the general layout of the development, the architect is a key member of your professional team, and usually one of the first members to get involved at the project inception phase.

Architects draw the original plans and submit them to the planners, and once you get planning permission approved they draw the working drawings. Working drawings are like comprehensive instruction manuals with details of every single screw, nut, nail, bolt and piece of wood, setting out where everything goes and how the builders should build. Architects who produce good drawings are worth their weight in gold because good drawings enable efficient construction. Architects also get involved in project management by making sure that the builder and main contractors are building what they have designed correctly. The architect will choose every material and the planners will probably insist on having full details before they grant planning permission.

> " Architects who produce good drawings are worth their weight in gold "

Beware – a lot of architects want to be the next Frank Lloyd Wright but they don't realise, or perhaps don't care, what things cost. Copper roofs, aluminium-plated external cladding, reflective smoked glass, or an intricate design detail might look cool in their heads and on paper, but unusual materials and complicated detailing can cost a fortune. Before you agree to any design, you should ask yourself, is it going to add value to my building? Will my clients want this? Architects do get carried away, and you have to be the person who stops them from getting out of control.

Architect's fees are around 4–5 per cent of the value of the construction contract. For complex projects, fees may increase to 6–8 per cent, which may be negotiable.

The structural engineer

Responsible for designing the foundations of your new buildings and ensuring their stability, the structural engineer plays an important role in bigger projects. The structural engineer will finalise the structural side. Will it be a steel or concrete frame? How will the roof sit? How do the foundations go in? How deep should the piles be driven? The engineer makes sure that the building will stand up and stay up. Engineers are very important as they design all the steel joists and structural components. They liaise with the architect, and make sure your building is built correctly.

The fees of a structural engineer are around 1.5–2.5 per cent of the contract value.

The quantity surveyor

The quantity surveyor (or cost engineer or construction cost consultant) is the person who ensures that the cost estimates, cash flow, and the development, is in accordance with the budget. The quantity surveyor should also be able to advise on contracts. They can calculate how much a construction should cost, no matter how big, so that when your proposal goes out to tender, you know roughly what it is going to cost you. Your quantity surveyor and the main contractor will have a debate about all the items and you will eventually agree a price that both sides are happy with. The quantity surveyor will monitor the project throughout its lifecycle. Their fees range from 1.5–2 per cent of the value of the construction project.

The landscape designer

A landscape designer should be consulted for any size or type of scheme. Planning permission for a project usually includes a condition requiring the submission and approval of a landscaping scheme before the development commences.

You can get a landscape designer to give you basic advice for just a few hundred pounds, or you can get them to do a very detailed scheme and manage the work through. They can advise on soft landscaping, planting, paving, street furniture, sculpture, etc. Designers are usually paid on a time basis.

> **The exterior is a key element in selling a property**

As mentioned on page 147, the exterior is a key element in selling a property. I have met people who swear their decision to buy a property is based on great landscaping and an inviting exterior.

In my experience, planners do not like large developments that require maintenance, such as grass. Grass needs to be cut, watered and maintained, which requires resources and energy. Planners press hard for a maintenance-free landscape such as hard landscaping with stones, slate, or wood chippings, but it can be difficult to make those landscapes look good. That's where landscape architects help; they will advise you on the right plants to enhance a building and create a charming environment.

The project manager

You might feel that you can manage your own project as you have all the other professionals in place, but I think it is important to delegate that responsibility if you can. Once you start working on bigger developments you need to be out and about finding deals and getting funds, rather than sitting on the site all day making sure that everything is going according to plan.

There are many companies that provide project managers. They can be expensive, so build them into your budget. Professional project managers will try to build in the quickest way at the best possible price and in the way you want it. A good project manager needs to be disciplined, efficient, good at figures, unflappable and used to dealing with personnel.

A dedicated project manager's fee might be between 1.5–4 per cent of construction costs, depending upon their precise role and the complexity of the project.

The total fees payable to the key members of the professional team are likely to be around 8 per cent of the total cost of the project for the most straightforward types of development, rising to 18 per cent or higher for complex projects.

2 Work in harmony

There are always going to be some disputes or fallings-out, and it is best to keep out of the way, unless it is something serious. Once, during a construction, we wanted a specific type of kitchen and delivery was delayed. The main contractor said that this delay was going to hold them back and so they would charge an extra £50,000. We argued very hard that it wouldn't actually hold them back as they could get on with other building work, but they said it did, so we had to compromise. Anything you have done that will hold back the main contractors will give them an opportunity to seek compensation. Many large contractors will price jobs to the bone and then make profits from what they call 'change orders' – the changes that are made to the contract through no fault of theirs.

> **There are always going to be some disputes or fallings-out** This is when a strong team of project manager, quantity surveyor, structural engineer and architect on your side plays a key role. They help to make sure that you and the main contractor have a realistic budget when the project commences. This should eliminate the chances of being hit with change orders, helping to maintain a good relationship with your contractor whilst keeping the project on budget.

3 Work with the Building Regulations department

Building Regulations have nothing to do with planning permission. A lot of people think that when they get planning permission they can build whatever they want, but Building Regulations are a totally separate department, and they ensure that your building is sound and structurally correct. Even when no planning permission is needed, Building Regulations may be required.

The types of work for which you must have Building Regulations approval include any extension, loft or cellar conversions, anything that affects the structure (such as the removal of load-bearing walls), relocation of bathrooms or kitchens, new heating appliances, underpinning, new windows, replacing roof covering, installation of cavity insulation, and the erection of new buildings.

> **Beware: if a property does not get building regulations approval, you may have to pull it down** In any development, whenever there are any structural changes or alterations, you have to get them signed off by the building control officer. Building control officers will inspect the work on a regular basis to make sure that everything is done according to the various standards and guidelines, and will point you in the right direction if something goes astray. If they think there are health and safety issues, they will call in the health and safety officers, and they have the power to close your site down immediately.

The process typically involves the following stages:

- You must complete the documentation and relevant application forms based on the guidelines issued by the local planning offices. Building Regulations are updated or amended from time to time and your builder needs to be conversant with the changes, via the architect.

- You will submit a building notice with detailed plans along with completed forms and fee.

- A building control officer will visit your site and any work that does not comply must be changed.

- A Building Regulations Approval Certificate will be issued when work is completed to their satisfaction.

There have been many cases where builders have been unable to get a certificate. If that happens, you will not be able to sell the property. The solicitors in due diligence cases will always want to see the building control sign-off certificates.

Value the judgement of the building control officers and their skills. We all need safe buildings.

Let's assume that you've used your wealth team and created your property. I assume that you know your marketplace, but you need to be flexible. Property markets change rapidly or maybe your circumstances have changed. A huge dilemma for all developers arises as you near the end of your project. Am I going to sell this? Or am I going to hold onto it and build up an investment portfolio? Well, I like to add value, sell and get out, but maybe that doesn't suit you, so let's have a look at what your next move is.

14

What are you going to do – hold or sell?

...this is a more important decision than you think!

Growing a business involves making difficult decisions. What are you going to do with your newly developed property? This is the question that most developers face as they come to the end of their project. Should you hold and rent or should you sell and release the equity? This really is an important question and it's one only *you* can answer because only *you* know your circumstances. For me, it's a simple decision. I like to crystallise my profit and sell. I can utilise my profits because I'm motivated to find new projects.

However, if you have a more passive approach to your property portfolio you might want to hold onto your property as a rental investment. Here are the essentials:

1 Should you rent it out?

2 Assess the local information: transport, education, employment, environment

3 Do your yield calculations

4 Managing your cash flow

1 Should you rent it out?

This can be a really appealing option; you get a return from renting, and if the market goes up, the capital value of the property increases. The problem is that it ties up your equity, and slows you down from moving on to another project. However, if you want to become a property developer, then you most likely need to sell, releasing the equity to move onto your next project.

This book is about becoming a property developer, not a landlord. If you rent your property you will have an income stream but little capital – you put a ceiling on how far you can climb. If you decide to become a landlord, you need different skills, including finding good tenants, using agencies, property maintenance, and understanding income tax. That's all perhaps, for another book!

If you are a small landlord there are many potential tenant disasters – they refuse to pay rent, they create unexpected repairs, and do moonlight flits, leaving you with an empty property. Perhaps this matters less to large landlords where you can factor in a certain amount of difficult tenants to your business plan. If you manage the property yourself you need to be prepared for a call at midnight from a tenant who wants a new light bulb. If you have a management company, they may charge up to 17.5 per cent of your rent in management fees. Don't forget that you are also going to be paying tax on your income.

> **This book is about becoming a property developer, not a landlord**

If you sell your property you don't have the risk of the market dropping or being left with rental voids and tenant trouble.

2 Assess the local information

There are sometimes good reasons to hold onto your property for a limited period. In my view, I don't believe that you can second-guess the global market (if you can, you should tell the Chancellor of the Exchequer). I don't think you can estimate how much property might rise or fall, in general. But you can use local information that will help you make the decision to sell or hold onto your property in the short-term. When deciding whether to hold, rent, or sell, take local factors into account:

- Transport

- Education

- Employment

- Environment

If you bought your development with a view to selling when the local transport had improved, you might decide to wait until a new tube has opened, or the new tram is in place. The local price will not increase until the actual transport is in place and working. While the transport links are being installed, you can rent your property short-term, ready to sell when its potential is realised.

Perhaps you have noticed a change in the local school boundaries, or maybe a new Trust school is about to open in your locality. Education is a prime motivator for families who will pay over-the-odds to be in the right catchment area. While you wait for the Trust school to open, you can rent out your family house.

Look also at the drivers of local employment – maybe a new computer company is opening nearby – it will need to employ young IT professionals, and they will need somewhere to live. Alternatively,

" Use local information to help you make the decision to sell or hold "

perhaps a factory is closing – my friend Mike owned a flat near a gin distillery that he was renting to tenants. Gin creates a rather disgusting smell, and the locality was distinctly whiffy! He knew the factory would close, and when it did, he sold – at a good profit.

The question I always consider is, 'If I leave my money in this scheme, will I get a better return than if I take it out and invest it in another project?' The answer is usually that I will get a better return actively developing property, as opposed to passively investing over the long-term.

3 Do your yield calculations

If you decide to hold onto your property, you must do a yield calculation. A study of yields will show that they vary wildly – surprisingly, a beautiful house in a smart street may not make as big a yield as an apartment in a poorer area. Rents do not swing as much as property prices, and have a narrower band; the person renting does not see an appreciation of the asset, so doesn't expect to pay the value of the asset. In some areas, there is an over-supply of rented properties, which makes the rent vulnerable to change. Your yield calculation will need to include what landlords call 'the void' – this is the time that the property stands empty between tenants.

So, let's look at hold versus sell and what it means in reality. This is my rule of thumb to work out the profit margins on hold or sell. You can use this model to run your own figures. Don't forget, you are always looking for a 25 per cent profit on all your deals and you need to factor in how the local market for property is moving. In the examples on the chart over the page I have used a market growth of 10 per cent, of course this is just an assumption – as they say in the advertisements, the market can go down as well as up!

After only three years you can build your equity up to £241k at a modest 20 per cent return on capital.

Renting (even in a good market giving a 10 per cent return or yield) doesn't give you anything like the profit you can make if you take your equity out each time and start again. Even with a small profit, the cash that you take out allows you to borrow more from the bank. Using my formula you should always make a 25 per cent+ return on your investment, so the more you can borrow for your next deal, the more money you can make.

If the economic conditions take a downturn, cash is even more valuable. Remember, because you have sold your property rather

WHAT IF...

Let's assume you have now completed your project at a total cost of **£100k**.

YOU SELL

- You can sell now for **£120k** and release your initial equity of £30k (for example) + profit of £20k (20 per cent ROCE), so you now have total equity of **£50k**.

YOU RENT

- You could rent out your property for **£730** per month (for example). Assuming the market goes up by **10 per cent** per annum, the next three years look like this (assuming rent covers mortgage/fees/maintenance, etc.):

- Value of Property at end of Year 1 = £132,000

- Value of Property at end of Year 2 = £145,200

- Value of Property at end of Year 3 = £159,720

(Note: you can also re-mortgage to release some equity)

- Over three years at 10 per cent growth per annum that £50k of equity is now worth £89.7k (an increase of £39.7k).

YOU RE-INVEST

- However, if you take the £50k and invest it in several development schemes, working to my formula the profit is as follows:

- **Scheme 1:** With your £50k equity you can borrow at least £167k. If you then invest this sum and sell your next property for £200k = Profit £41k + equity £50k (Total £91k)

- **Scheme 2:** Costs £300K, sell for £360k = Profit £60k + equity £91k (Total £151k)

- **Scheme 3:** Costs £450K, sell for £540k = Profit £90k + equity £151k (Total £241k) than holding onto it as a rental investment, you have crystallised your profits, thus no one can take them away from you. So the trick is to bank your money, take a fresh look at the market, and move onto your next deal. In my mind, pro-active always beats passive. But this is your call, depending on your circumstances.

4 Managing your cash flow

Cash flow is the key to success or failure in this game, especially in this market. Don't forget to include your own living expenses if you are planning to do property development full time. You still have to pay your own rent/mortgage, bills, food, etc!

● Plan your budget meticulously. Itemise in detail the things you will have to apply for, and buy. Calculate on the pessimistic side to avoid nasty shocks.

● Be realistic about what you can take on financially.

● Make sure you can definitely access the money for the purchase and other expenses.

● Keep detailed records to calculate the tax you will need to pay. You can offset some costs (ask your local tax office for guidelines).

● Review your calculations regularly as the work progresses.

Now you've decided if you are going to sell or hold. Either way, you've got to make sure that you market your property in the best possible manner. Marketing your property is important because the more money you make, the bigger investment you can put into your next development. So what are the essential elements of marketing and selling?

15

Marketing and selling property

...always aim for the highest possible return!

Getting the best possible return on a property development depends on how well you market it – people want to buy into what they perceive to be success. Their idea of their lifestyle is expressed by the home they own. When you sell a property you are really selling people a dream of a cool lifestyle; people pay top prices because they want to live the dream. If you have decided to sell your property, you will be determined to achieve the best possible price. This is going to depend on your marketing skills. Before you bought the property you made a sales assessment and had a clear idea about the kind of person you would sell to. Then you renovated and refurbished the property to meet every want, need, and expectation of your future buyers; now is the time to realise that potential.

Let's look at the ways to market and sell the dream property you have developed. Here are the essentials:

1 Work with estate agents: get three to value your property

2 Sell your property yourself

3 Choose your timing: March to May are the best months

4 Sell the lifestyle

5 Use brochures and 'for sale' signs

6 Prepare for viewings

7 Be ready to accept offers

1 Work with estate agents

Contact three reputable estate agents based in your area, and arrange appointments for all the agents to value the property on the same day. Ask to see comparable prices, but try and be realistic about your asking price. You should be wary of an agent who gives an inflated estimate; try not to be flattered by the highest valuation. In reality, the property is worth only what a buyer is willing to pay for it.

Once you've chosen an agent, you need to build a good rapport with them. As with any relationship, if estate agents like and respect you, they'll do more to help sell your property. Commission is usually between 0.5–2.25 per cent for sole agency and 1–3 per cent for joint agency. Agree a contract time of 4–12 weeks, so you can change agency if you feel they are not working effectively.

Communication with your estate agent is crucial to the sales process. Agree a specific time to discuss progress every week, and keep in touch on a regular basis. If you don't keep in contact, the estate agents can forget about your property. Of course, there is a fine line here – don't pester them, but quietly let them know that you're expecting updates every week.

> **Ask your agent for any negative feedback on your property**

Get feedback from your estate agent

Ask your estate agent for any negative feedback on your property. You need to be realistic about what it can achieve in terms of price, and why it's not selling. Sometimes the news about your property will not be what you want to hear. Work together to overcome any shortcomings. Attack is the best form of defence. Ask your agent to make a point of saying, 'Yes, we know this property doesn't have the car parking you asked for, but the reason that it doesn't is because . . . you can get residents parking/we are right beside the tube station/there is plenty of parking in nearby streets . . .' Your potential buyers will be planning their own future sale, so you need to give them peace of mind on any issues that come up.

When you ask for negative feedback, the agent might give you something that you can change, such as 'If you open that curtain, paint the wall, or you move this piece of furniture, you'd make it look better.' Take their advice.

The average time it takes to sell a property is six weeks from the first viewing. If after six weeks you've had between a dozen and twenty viewings and you've had no offers, you know your price is too high. You really don't want to start putting prices down, but if it's too high, it's too high.

> **There's a price that it will sell for in seconds, and there's a price that it won't sell for**

If you think about anything that you buy and sell, there's a price that it will sell for in seconds, and there's a price that it won't sell for. Nine times out of ten, if something doesn't shift, it's usually because of price – your property price needs to reflect your location, your specification, and the market expectation. Sometimes you have to sell for less than you think the property is worth, but time is money in this game, and if you are making a profit, then get on with it!

② Sell your property yourself

There are two main benefits to selling your own property – you cut out the middleman, and keep the commission fee in your own pocket. Five per cent of people in the UK buy and sell their own homes, and the research claims that if you sell your own home you can sell it faster and for more money, because no one can sell something like the owner. That doesn't mean estate agents are to be ignored – they're at the crux of the whole property market – but there are great opportunities for working independently on-line. If you think you are the type of person who can sell your own property, my advice is to use a property website, but also use an estate agent.

As previously mentioned, it is fair to say that a lot of people don't trust estate agents. They've been accused of inflating prices and conning people, not to mention telling lies about properties, so many purchasers feel that if they have got the opportunity to go direct to the seller, they can get a straight deal at a better price.

One issue is letting strangers into your property. Estate agents will vet buyers, do the viewings, and they are insured. If this concerns you, get a friend to help, or do one full day of viewings. You can vet potential buyers by email, asking them to send references or their work address.

3 Choose your timing

Timing is everything. Statistically, the best time to sell is between March and May, as spring inspires and motivates people. When there are more people looking, you get better prices. In spring, people are interested in starting afresh, and finding a new place to live. Usually Easter is a really strong time for selling, too. September is also considered a strong month, after the main holiday season. August, November, December, January and February are known as the slowest months. It's worth bearing in mind that when you are buying, rather than selling, the reverse applies – a great time to buy is always November and December. People who sell in November want to get their property sold before the New Year, so you can usually get incredible bargains. The middle of summer is very slack, with buyers away on holiday.

" The best time to sell is April and May, as spring inspires and motivates people "

4 Sell the lifestyle

Marketing is not just about selling your property; marketing is about selling a lifestyle. The person that wants to buy your property needs to imagine what it will be like to live in it.

If your potential buyer is moving up the property ladder, they want to aspire to a new life. Your property has to hold the promise of improving their quality of life, and make them look better to their friends. If you can promote the property as sophisticated, it will sell faster. For example, I try to put a computer and a desk in the property (even if it's in the hall) so people can see they can work from home. A flat screen television, a clean, bright, decluttered style, and well-designed kitchen and bathroom are important.

Estate agents used to tell us that the smell of baking bread and coffee would help sell a property, but I believe having a couple of bottles of champagne and a Porsche brochure lying on the table is just as successful.

5 Use brochures and 'for sale' signs

A property brochure can be helpful marketing. This is your selling platform; you are inviting interested customers to learn more about what you are selling. It must be carefully constructed and expertly printed. Make it your mission to produce the highest quality brochure possible. You can design it on your computer, but don't do anything low quality, as you never want to look desperate to sell.

For a larger development, without doubt, you need your own brochure. It gives you credibility. It's your chance, sell the lifestyle associated with your property. You can use it alongside a factual estate agent's brochure. You will notice that property developer's brochures are all about lifestyles. They will have a gorgeous woman on the front with a good-looking guy drinking champagne and laughing. The aim is to sell your property quickly, and for the most money. Remember to take a step back and ask yourself, Will this sell my property quicker? Will this

> **The aim is to sell your property quickly, and for the most money**

help me get the best price? Distribute your brochures to neighbours to help generate 'word of mouth'. Arrange an open day and advertise it in your local paper or via the Internet. Have brochures ready to give to viewers.

Sales boards

Agents will ask you if you want a 'for sale' board put up outside your house – estate agents claim that 70 per cent of sales comes from signs, so it is hugely important. Some agents leave their boards up too long; if there are lots of boards up in your road, make sure the agents take them down, because potential buyers will wonder why there are so many properties for sale in the street, and worry that there is something wrong with the area.

6 Prepare for viewings

Whether you are selling the property yourself, or working with an agent, you need to prepare for viewings. You need to be in the mindset of selling – especially if you are living in the property. If you are working through an agent ask them to give plenty of notice of when someone's going to look at it. Your property has to look like a show home all the time.

Treat each and every telephone call as though you are talking to a potential buyer. Gain as much information as you can, be prepared to supply information, be aware that not all callers are genuine, and book your viewing appointments at a time that will show your property under best possible conditions.

Make sure your property is clean and tidy. If people come in and see washing everywhere you're giving them a negative impression. If you are doing the viewings yourself, welcome viewers with a smile. Think about which rooms to show them first and last; make them rooms to remember. Don't rush viewings.

> " Your property has to look like a show home all the time "

7 Be ready to accept offers

At this point, you should be in a good position to receive an offer on the property. Be wary of aggressive cash buyers because sometimes they try and get your property for peanuts, and keep calm during negotiations. Assess the strength and quality of a buyer, aim high with your price, but be prepared to compromise. Never appear too keen to sell.

When you receive offers on your property, keep cool during negotiations. Estate agents are a good buffer between you and the potential purchaser. If the purchaser is not happy with the asking price, they can deal with the estate agent, and you don't have to deal with them directly.

If you are going to sell the property yourself, sometimes it's good to get someone else to negotiate for you, and take a more objective view. Have a competent solicitor ready. Remember, when there is good money on the table, take it!

16

Your twelve-week property plan

...it's time to get started...no excuses!

I want to challenge you because research has shown that 97 per cent of people reading books like this never take action. They don't take the next step. Now I'm going to embarrass you, even pressure you into taking the next step. I want you now, armed with the information I've given you, to go out and build a property portfolio of your own!

Remember, there are thousands of property deals to be done, as long as you can get your hands on the finance. It's time to get up off your butt and go for it! You can take the steps to become a property success in the next twelve weeks. You can do this alongside your current job and some of the more ambitious of you may actually buy and refurb and sell within the twelve weeks, but this is a good guide to get you started.

A lot of you may think that you can do this easily, but sometimes finding the life-changing deal can take what feels like years, rather than three months. It is possible to find your deal in three months. I know it can be done because many people who have attended my seminars are following my twelve-week property plan and are on the road to riches already – many of them within six weeks, never mind twelve.

The hardest step is the first step. Think about this. What is the toughest part of anything? You see the world's strongest man pulling a lorry with his teeth. What's the toughest part? The toughest part isn't in the middle, or towards the end. The toughest part is getting started. That's where you need to put the most strength, energy and focus. The hardest part is actually getting up and doing it. We hear rags to riches stories every day of the week; now you've just got to do it. So now is the time to start the 12-week Property Plan. I am giving you a twelve-week timeframe, so get out your diary and get started.

Week 1   Set your goals

Let's assume that today is the day you are going to start to make money from property. The first thing to do is set your life goals and objectives – not just that you want to be rich (don't we all!) but what you really want from life. You may have thought about this already, but now is the moment to write down your three main goals. The purpose of writing down your goals and objectives is to take a step back and ask, 'Do I really want to get into this? Is this the type of thing that I'm cut out to do?' You need to be very careful – this is your life and only you will know if this is how you want to spend your time.

" You've got to be prepared for living in absolute chaos for your first two or three developments "

If you have written down, 'meet a perfect partner and have a baby', or 'play tennis to Wimbledon standard', then maybe property development is not for you. This is a really tough game; it's not for the fainthearted. If you go ahead you will be in a business where every step you take will be expensive – the banks have rising interest rates, the taxman will take money from you, and of course, personal cash flow is very challenging.

You've got to be prepared for living in absolute chaos for your first two or three developments. If they are your primary residence, you will be the person without water or heating when the plumber doesn't turn up; you will be the person covered in brick dust when the wall is knocked down to put on the extension; and you will be the person worrying about cash flow in a falling market. You've got to be robust and be able to get up when you get knocked down.

Write down:

● How much you have to invest and what do you want to do in the first year? Is your aim to sell one property in the first six months?

● What type of property are you going to develop? Do you want to develop a one-bedroom flat and make a £20,000 profit? Or do a house and make a £40,000 profit? Or do two apartments?

- Where are you going to look for property?

- When do you want to start? Will you structure a property development business right away?

- How much money do you expect to make?

Be specific with your answers. Include dates. Write down your aims for the next twelve weeks. Your aims must be measurable so there is a clear roadmap of what you need to do. Put specific dates in your diary and work to them. This is the start of your business plan. Many of the activities (finding a property, negotiating and raising money) run in unison, so you are going to be busy.

Think about your life

Are you going to live in your property? Are you going to stay in your job as you start on the ladder of property development? How much work can you do in the evenings after your usual workday? Understand your parameters; you're only human, what can you push yourself to? Can you really do another apartment when you're working in an office during the day? What can you achieve, and when?

Think about your wealth team

Collect together the contact details for the people you will need. These people are part of your business plan, so make a list of who are going to help form your property development team.

Weeks 2–4 Find your life-changing deal

You're now going to look for a property. In week one, you have identified your goals, objectives and type of property you want to find. Search every single option to try and find it; walk the streets, call estate agents, read property papers, go to auctions and don't come up with excuses that 'there's nothing out there'. There are loads of good properties available. There are always deals, everywhere, and you are going to find one.

Start a database; list the property deals you have looked at and why they weren't for you. Build up an analysis of what could work for the future. Over the course of the first few weeks, you can find your life-changing deal.

Week 5   Make sure the deal works

Carry out this initial checklist for every property you visit:

- [ ] Is it leasehold or freehold?
- [ ] What is the area like? Is it up and coming, are there skips on the road, and what are the neighbours like? Research the crime statistics, schools, shops, and cafés.
- [ ] Assess the building. Inspect the structure, walls, floors, roofs, and state of repair.
- [ ] Decide if this is a makeover or refurbishment. Work out ballpark budget.
- [ ] Can you get the property for at least 25 per cent below market value, or can you add some serious value?
- [ ] Consider who is going to buy or rent your property once you have developed it.
- [ ] Prepare your basic residual valuation and do your due diligence.
- [ ] Does it meet your time scale?
- [ ] Does it stack up financially?

Avoid paralysis by analysis. Don't become one of those people who never stop checking, checking, checking, and fail to make a decision. Gut feeling is important as well. Few properties tick every box.

Week 6   Focus, choose and offer

Compile a shortlist of the properties that fulfil your criteria. On average, you should have analysed at least 30+ properties to find one that works.

If a property ticks every box and you know you are getting it at a great price, it's worth trying to buy it immediately. My advice is to go with it, and if it turns out to be 'too good to be true' let it go (however, don't make a habit of this!). When you are certain of the property you want to purchase, put in an offer right away. Procrastination is a property developer's downfall, so don't mess around. When you have decided to buy, move fast, because in my experience, there's always someone trying to pick up that bargain, too.

Week 7   Know what you are buying

Take off any rose-tinted glasses and look at this property on a worst-case basis:

- Are there hidden problems?
- What's the exit strategy?
- Will the values hold up?
- Will anyone buy it?
- Why is it so cheap?
- What if I can't sell it?

Prepare a detailed residual valuation; know that your deal works, and that you can defend the deal to anyone.

Weeks 8–10   Get the funding

I am giving you two weeks for this because finding the funding is just like finding the deal; it's out there (although, in reality you will be teeing up on finance from day one). You may need to create a clear business plan to show that you can make a profit. Present your proposals, projected cash flow, timescale, specification, and market research.

Line up a mortgage or a bank loan, or talk to your investors – or a mixture of these. Meet with banks, call financial advisors, and mortgage companies. Search all options to get the funding agreed.

Start the detailed due diligence. Ask your solicitor to carry out the searches and various checks to ensure good title. Once funding has been agreed, the lenders will require the appropriate surveys, ensuring that what they are lending money on actually stacks up.

Weeks 11–12   Make the profit

Exchange with up to a maximum of a 10 per cent deposit and complete the deal thereafter. This is when you make a profit; you make your money when you buy, NOT when you sell!

Now, proceed with your chosen strategy: are you going to sell or let? Makeover or refurbish? Do your own project management? It's all in this book, so make sure you make the right decisions.

If you have followed the formula, and you have ticked all the boxes, you will sell or hold your development, and make a profit of at least 20 per cent on the total capital.

The future

Now, start looking for your next development project. I have taken you through the whole property process: you found a property, you bought it, you've added value, you've decided to hold it or sell it, you've got the price you want . . . now it's time to start the cycle again.

If you get your deal right, you sell your property, and then you loop back to the start again. If you have completed the steps in this book you should be in the process of looking for your next property. The more deals you get on the go, the closer you are to making serious money from property.

I don't know how long it's going to take you to read the 12-week Property Plan; say 15 minutes? Well, you are now 15 minutes into your twelve weeks. But before you get too excited, let me remind you to avoid the mistakes that amateurs make time and time again.

17

Avoid the classic mistakes

...don't take your eye off the ball!

Even the most confident and experienced property developers still make mistakes. If you take your eye off the ball, or you make a decision without thinking, it doesn't matter how big you are, or how successful you've been in the past, things can go wrong.

In this chapter I will be telling you what the classic mistakes are, so that you can avoid them. And if you do make a mistake, pick yourself up, fix it or worst case – start again.

Here are the essentials:

1 Don't buy on a railway track

2 Don't be afraid to take a risk

3 Don't limit your horizons

4 Don't get upset by rejections or setbacks

5 Don't work alone

6 Believe in yourself

7 Keep on your toes: be flexible, things change

8 The Pareto principle (the 80/20 rule)

9 Don't waste time

10 Have fun!

1 Don't buy on a railway track

I have a friend, Steve, who bought a beautiful flat near Waterloo station in London on a new development. It was a one-bed flat on the ground floor with a garden and it was gorgeous – he couldn't believe the price he got it for. Looking back, he realised he only viewed the flat at bizarre times. The developer selling the property was never available when he wanted to view. Anyway, he moved in and suddenly the flat started shaking. Steve opened the door to the back garden and the noise just kept getting louder and louder. Whoosh, the Eurostar train rushed by. The Eurostar was literally 10 metres from the end of his back garden. It was going past every half an hour. He was devastated. He put it on the market and ended up losing money when he sold it. The point is that you can tick all the boxes, but things can go wrong. So check, double check and check again.

> **"If just one thing is not right, you can end up losing a lot of money"**

2 Don't be afraid to take a risk

The first mistake of an amateur property developer is that they will not take calculated risks. You have to trust your gut feeling and take your first leap of faith in buying a property. Do your due diligence, but know that you are taking a calculated chance. A downturn in the market creates great opportunities to find bargains, if you are not risk averse. Use the formula in this book to make a valued judgement, and then take a calculated risk. Whatever you do, don't become a spectator. Get on the pitch and play ball!

3 Don't limit your horizons

The next common mistake is thinking small. Yes, you will be starting modestly, but you still need to think big. It takes almost as much effort to refurbish a small property as it does a big one. If you are buying and adding value to several properties you will find economies of scale. The profit margin on a large deal is higher than the profit margin on a small deal. Think big and your deals will create their own momentum.

4 Don't get upset by rejections or setbacks

Studies have shown that, on average, it takes 20 years to become a millionaire. Apparently, Richard Branson did not have any disposable income until he was 43. As I told you in the introduction, it took me three years to make my first million; but in reality I had spent ten years in corporate and five years at university learning my trade. It has been a 20 year process. I have had to handle rejection from banks and have dealt with setbacks; it happens to us all.

5 Don't work alone

I suggest you find a mentor. Look for an experienced, highly regarded, empathetic person to guide you. Ideally, this will be someone who knows property development and can help you re-examine your own ideas for your business. Your mentor will help your personal and professional development. You can find mentors through introductions at business networking events, or friends who have become successful. Or you might read about famous entrepreneurs such as Richard Branson or Alan Sugar whose ideas, concepts and energy will help you get to the next level.

Your support team also includes your partner, your family and your friends. They will listen to your stories of deals that you just missed, and then be with you to celebrate when you sell your first property at a profit.

Then there are two other groups of people who are important for your success – your employees and your customers. Foster good relationships with both, and it will make property development a more enjoyable and successful process. If in doubt, use this book, attend my seminars, and get as much inspiration as you can to take the next step.

6 Believe in yourself

The classic mistake of the amateur is to underestimate his or her own ability. Remember, you can make money. It may sound a bit cheesy, but you must believe in yourself. In today's fast-moving society perception is reality; how your colleagues and customers perceive you is vital for your business. You need to take a long, hard look at your own identity. If you were a brand, what would it be? Even if, like me, you have to spend days stripping woodchip paper off the walls of your property as you refurbish it, your identity is not just a scruffy builder; you are a property entrepreneur and business developer.

Many amateurs are frightened of raising their profile. You may think that because I have presented television shows that I enjoy publicity. Actually, I find it quite challenging, and it is hard work, but it has got an upside. You need to tell everyone what you are doing – word of mouth recommendation is the best publicity you can get. You cannot buy a great reputation. If someone likes your work, such as an estate agent or a builder, and tells someone else, then your business starts to grow.

" You need to tell everyone what you are doing "

Pay attention to new media opportunities – the Internet represents a great opportunity to connect with anyone, anywhere, and you can build your own website to publicise your business.

7 Keep on your toes

How are you going to continue to provide the best and keep on improving? Life doesn't stop because you have made a profit on one property sale. When you go round the loop again, maybe the property market will have moved further, and it will be even more important to offer great service and a top-quality, high-specification property to ensure that you maximise profit. To stay on top, you cannot sit still, you must continually improve. Onwards and upwards is the only way.

Nothing stays the same. Just when you think you know what you are doing, there is a new set of building issues on the horizon. You need to be flexible, and be prepared to totally change your strategy. You might need to diversify to give yourself as many chances as possible. If you have been successful with one-bedroom city apartments, now might be the time to move to large country houses. Keep on your toes.

8 The Pareto principle

Also known as the 80–20 rule, the Pareto principle states that, on average, 20 per cent of what you do achieves 80 per cent of the results. For example, 20 per cent of a sales force will achieve 80 per cent of sales, and 20 per cent of your customers provide 80 per cent of your turnover.

You need to identify the 20 per cent, and increase it. If you can increase it to 40 per cent, you will achieve 160 per cent of what you did before.

It sounds simple, but, of course, it is not. What you need is focus. It is hard when you are starting out, and you need to watch every detail, but if you can step back for a moment and try and work out what kind of property development in your area will create the most revenue, you are getting closer to understanding how to make your first million.

9 Don't waste time

Focus will help you avoid the most common amateur mistake – time wasting. These are examples of time-wasting activities; make sure you don't do them:

- Poor delegation
- Delayed decisions
- Poor communication
- Poor self-discipline

10 Have fun!

Make sure you enjoy the ride. This is meant to be fun, okay, it is going to be very challenging and stressful at times – but you've got to enjoy the journey, that's what it's all about.

So there you have it. You're armed with all the information you need – what to do, and what not to do to be successful – it's time for us to let you get on with it!

Just do it!

...money is by no means everything, but believe me, it makes life easier!

But remember, the key to making money from property is that you don't expect to make it all in one go – unlike winning the lottery – it doesn't come in one lump sum, but get the formula right and it can mount up quickly. I have shown you all the steps to develop property and make a healthy profit. On the first deal you might make a ten grand profit – good, you are now on the way. You then reinvest the ten grand for the next deal, and you will be pushing for the 20 per cent plus return. As you do more deals you will make more profits.

People say that money alone does not make you happy and that is certainly true. However, it does bring financial security, which means you don't have to worry about paying the mortgage, bills and school fees, you can buy a nice car, live in a great house, go on wonderful holidays and help the people you care about – including supporting any charities that you are particularly close to. It really is worth working hard for your money and don't feel guilty about it, you deserve to be rich!

You can see in your calculations that if you do three, four, or five of these deals within a short period of time you can quickly reach your goals, it's a snowball effect. If you keep going you can take it even further. It's really up to you how far you want to push it, but remember it only takes one great deal to change your life. When I was starting my business I built up the deals slowly. One day a bank asked me for an asset statement and, to my surprise, I found that I was worth over a million. It had taken me over three years and I haven't looked back since. The first million is without doubt the hardest to make, but you have to be patient, it is built up from lots of small deals. The good news is that if you follow my example and grow your business successfully, in the future just one deal could make you many millions!

Be confident in your own ability and when you find an obstacle in your path, keep going, because if it was easy everyone would be doing it.

Nonetheless, there are thousands of people out there, including myself, making a great living out of property every day, so believe me it is possible. I've received countless e-mails, letters and cards from people who started from nothing and who are quickly becoming property entrepreneurs, even in these difficult times.

Now it's your turn to take it to the next level and to put the theory into practice, so go make it happen, beat the credit crunch, don't listen to the cynics... and just do it!

Index

Useful Information:

My website: www.garymccausland.com
NMP Management
PO Box 981
Wallington
Surrey
SM6 8JU
Tel: 020 8669 3128

Royal Institution of Chartered Surveyors
RICS Contact Centre
Surveyor Court
Westwood Way
Coventry
CV4 8JE
Tel: 087 0333 1600
Website: www.rics.org

Royal Institute of British Architects
RIBA Client Services
66 Portland Place
London
W1B 1AD
Tel: 020 7307 3700
Website: www.ribafind.org

Citizens Advice Bureau
Myddelton House
115-123 Pentonville Road
London
N1 9LZ
Website: www.citizensadvice.org.uk

Institute of Structural Engineers
11 Upper Belgrave Street
London
SW12 8BH
Tel: 020 7235 4535
Website: www.istructe.org.uk

National Federation of Builders
55 Tufton Street
London
SW1P 3QL
Tel: 087 0898 9091
Website: www.builders.org.uk

The Federation of Master Builders
Gordon Fisher House
14-15 Great James Street
London
WC1N 3DP
Tel: 020 7242 7583
Website: www.fmb.org.uk

Painting and Decoratoring Association
32 Coton Road
Nuneaton
Warwickshire
CV11 5TW
Tel: 024 7635 3776
Website:
www.paintingdecoratingassociation.co.uk

Electrical Contractors Association
Head Office
ECA
ESCA House
34 Palace Court
London
W2 4HY
Tel: 020 7313 4800
Website: www.eca.co.uk

The Property Makeover Price Guide:
from BCIS
12, Great George Street, Parliament
Square, London SW1P 3 AD